T0067932

SCARRED

A JOURNEY OF RESTORATION

JAN LEVINE

WESTBOW
PRESS®
A DIVISION OF THOMAS NELSON
& ZONDERVAN

Scripture quotations taken from the New American Standard Bible® (NASB), Copyright © 1960, 1962, 1963, 1968, 1971, 1972, 1973, 1975, 1977, 1995 by The Lockman Foundation Used by permission. www.Lockman.org

WestBow Press books may be ordered through booksellers or by contacting:

WestBow Press
A Division of Thomas Nelson & Zondervan
1663 Liberty Drive
Bloomington, IN 47403
www.westbowpress.com
1 (866) 928-1240

Because of the dynamic nature of the Internet, any web addresses or links contained in this book may have changed since publication and may no longer be valid. The views expressed in this work are solely those of the author and do not necessarily reflect the views of the publisher, and the publisher hereby disclaims any responsibility for them.

Any people depicted in stock imagery provided by Thinkstock are models, and such images are being used for illustrative purposes only. Certain stock imagery © Thinkstock.

ISBN: 978-1-5127-8771-9 (sc)
ISBN: 978-1-5127-8772-6 (e)

Print information available on the last page.

WestBow Press rev. date: 5/25/2017

"You were dealt a losing hand," my uncle once expressed. He was right. My past seemed to be laid out in such a way that it always terminated in a dead end. I ran away from that dead end, seeking to find a place where I would discover love and acceptance. Unfortunately, running away brought more hardships. While there were many times I wanted to give up and physically die, it was not until I laid down my life before the throne of God, that I was dealt a new hand. My dead end was transformed into a narrow, but ever so long-lasting road. I am writing this story to share how I have learned, through a lot of hard work, to overcome the dysfunction that used to control me. My story, though, is not just *my story*, as it is intertwined with many others. Therefore, I have changed all names, including my own, to protect the privacy of others.

ACKNOWLEDGMENTS

Thank you Bekah Mason for how you found time to work closely with my story in the midst of all that you do so that it truly glorified God. Joanna Walter, this story would not have turned into the butterfly it is without your heart beating through the whole thing. Sarah Ryan, you bless me more than words can describe! Racheal Ndei, Marybeth Pritchard, Linda Hagg, Karol Joseph, Nicole Parramore, and Goldie, thank you for your prayers, encouragement, and reading of the manuscript at different stages, which made an absolute difference. I don't believe I would have had the courage to complete this very vulnerable transparent book without each of you coming along side me through this journey. What a blessing to have each of you in my life. In your own right, you're each true pillars of the faith.

Our time is short but the impact we can make is great so here's to the journey!

CONTENTS

INTRODUCTION

NEW BEGINNINGS

I can remember the first time that I opened a Christian Bible. It was much different from the Hebrew Bible I was used to. Bells didn't start ringing, and I didn't burn up, as I had often jokingly said would happen. I bought it the very first day I came to my new understanding of the God of Israel. I was thirty-one years old, and it was not the first time I was introduced to Jesus. However, it took many years, from the first time I heard about Jesus as the Messiah (as opposed to Jesus the anti-Semite) to believe.

The day I came to faith in Jesus, I was in a non-denominational church in Ft. Lauderdale, Florida. I had attended it ten years earlier, but this time was different. The church had a small bookstore, which I timidly walked into to purchase a Bible. I stood confused in front of the shelves containing a plethora of them. Little did I know they had Bible versions for everything and everyone. Standing there, I had no clue where to begin. I grew up in a Jewish home, and didn't even know the difference between Catholicism and Protestantism, let alone what to purchase. I must have looked like a deer staring into headlights on a dark, deserted road.

As I was reading all the different titles, a clerk approached me. She began speaking another language as she asked me things like "literal or paraphrased?" I just nodded, fearful of looking stupid, and leaned on an old saying I grew up hearing. "Fake it till you make it," my father would say. So that was what I did. After what seemed like an hour, I made it through the ordeal. I was shockingly excited that I had my new Bible. I could not wait to get home and open it. This was coming from a young lady who did not enjoy reading. There was most definitely something that changed inside of me that day, and my actions were already demonstrating that truth.

My journey since coming to faith that day has taught me to believe that we do not open the Bible to just any page and individually interpret what we think God is teaching us. I do believe, however, that when we genuinely lay down our lives to God, and admit that we need His guidance in understanding, He will show up even in our naivety. I was not even one day old in my faith, and I had no comprehension how to read the Word of God. I did not realize that it was the Word of God itself that would teach me how to understand, as opposed to reading it and understanding based on my own presumptions. Growing up Jewish, however, I knew to respect the Bible and never to take its words lightly.

Therefore, that day I opened my new Bible and prayed: "I have no clue what to do. I see where I have been, and I see where I am. Internally, there is nothing more in this life that I desire but to know You. Please guide me and instruct me in Your ways." There is no doubt that God showed up in that very moment, for the very first verse I opened up to was Psalm 118:8. I was ready for emotional stability in my life, and you will understand why as you read on. However, at that moment when I read, "It is better to trust in the Lord than to put confidence in man," I knew that God was calling me to let go of everything I was holding onto, and to learn how to walk with my eyes focused on Him above all that was around me. I may have had a sense of what God was up to in my life, but the long road ahead was unseen.

I share with you my first experience reading the Bible as a believer because that was the day my life changed in a way I never expected. If you do not believe in Jesus, you might be turned off by the mere mention of His name. I understand, because I spent thirty-one years of my life getting turned off by it. I still get turned off, not by the name of Jesus, but by Christians who preach at me as if they have arrived at some unique reality. I get upset when they give genuine believers a bad rap with their judgmental hypocrisy. However, I want you to know that I write this book because I believe that my story will touch the lives of men and women who struggle inwardly with their emotions and thoughts. My faith is part of my healing process, and it is something I can't leave out. I know with all my heart that what I have overcome is solely through the power of God.

See, my journey was hardcore before coming to faith, and a different type of hard afterward. In my past, I ran from the things that hurt me, and as a believer that habit tried to linger. The difference for me was, after I turned my heart to God, the love I was feeling for Him kept me from running.

Through a lot of hard work, God gave me biblical truths to hold onto, which I like to call tools. They allowed me to build a new structure in my life. I had been in traditional psychology and self-help groups since I was twelve years old, and they could only bandage my internal state. (I want to share a disclaimer here: I agree with the system of psychology for behavior modifications that are sometimes very much needed. I also believe that we are not just physical beings, and that there is more to us than just our behaviors.) There is something deeper than just action that transforms our behavior into what it is. My experiences and education have shown me that there is a root cause to every motive that hides behind our emotions and thought. It is ultimately those motives that produce our actions.

My circumstances had led me to embrace a codependent, self-defending way of dealing with life. That way only kept me in a constant state of internal struggles, unless I was high on some form of substance. I tried my best to deal with life sober, but my behavior began to push people out of my life. Even though I had once been the life of the party, I found myself unaccompanied by the time I came to faith. This was partially due to the choices I had begun to make a year prior. Needless to say, I spent the first seven years of my new walk as a believer in Jesus mostly in isolation. God did, however, perfectly place a few individuals here and there that took the time to get to know me and invest in me as a new believer.

During those first years, because I was so used to people wanting to be around me, I never understood why the majority of this new Christian world kept me at arm's length. I was terrified of this new world around me, and I struggled with feeling judged by most and unwanted by the rest. Surprisingly, I found more comfort in being solitary than being around others, so I refused to dwell on anything other than seeking to know God more. Today I see that those years in isolation were perfectly designed because I learned through that journey how to lean on God alone instead of my worth in the eyes of others. The verse that God had given me that very first day I opened my new Bible eventually became a lived-out reality.

Ultimately, God wanted me to heal from my past, and I had to learn how to trust in His perfect will. I have not reached some state of internal euphoria, but there *is* a real joy that remains whether I am alone or not. My integrity and my attitude toward God are most important to me now. Not how the world around me thinks that I am, and especially not whether or not someone wants me. It is remembering daily to uphold God at the center of my heart that has brought me to a place where I can address old dysfunctions that arise from time to time. As I mature, physically and spiritually, it becomes more second nature than something I am trying to develop. I am no longer running away, and by the power of God I have grown leaps and bounds in my emotional and mental condition. I can engage the world sober. This is the reason I want to invite you to journey through my life. To laugh, to cry, and to heal with me as we revisit how God has taught me how to allow Him to truly transform and renew my mind.

1

A MOTHER'S CHOICE

*I*t was a typical sunny South Florida day, as my memory recalls. It was the beginning of the school year, and I was only four years of age starting kindergarten. This was not because I was a genius at four; my birthday is in December, and the school year began in August. It is fun, though, to think it was due to the former reason. The year was 1978, and my parents had just divorced. My brother, who is older by four years, went to live with my father after days of protesting living with my mother. I was told he would stand in front of the window calling out for his dad day after day, so it was decided that that was best. I remained with my mother and her new boyfriend, who is now her husband of 35 years. Looking back, that may have seemed like the logical thing to do. Yet, if that were the case, I would probably not be writing this.

Returning from school one day, I got off the bus and my babysitter, who was always there, was not. Most children would be scared in this situation, especially at the age of four. Let me put this into perspective. Four years old ... that means I was just transitioning from infancy to childhood. I smile at my young self when I reflect on that moment. I must have been one of those children that people enjoyed watching as I demonstrated independence. Without crying or feeling lost, I knew immediately to walk to my babysitter's house. As I was passing my block on the way to her house, I naturally looked down the street with my young eyes to what seemed like a long road. I noticed that my mother's car was parked in front of our townhouse. That car brings up many memories. I called it, as I got older, "The Beast." It was this brown beaten down car with a sticker of Tweety Bird on the side. We would jam to Black Sabbath with the windows down, and she would pick up hitchhikers in it. I suppose times were different in the late 70s and early 80s, and my mother obviously had no sense of danger, even with me in the car. Eventually, a friend from her new crew of companions stole that car from her. I was told that she was left stranded at a 7-Eleven convenience store when that went down. When thinking about those experiences, I can only shake my head.

As I was walking to my babysitter's and I saw the car in our parking spot, it all began to make sense; my babysitter wasn't waiting for me because my mother was at home. All my love for my mom bubbled up into my heart, and I just could not wait to see her. I remember feeling extremely excited. I mean, after all, it was my mother, and she was home! At four years old, that was a big deal! I ran home so fast with such innocence in my motives, not realizing what was on the other side of the front door was about to alter my life and the way I would process everything. What happened next sums up the statement that expectations plus motives do not always produce the desired results. As I opened the front door, I remember my mother running up the staircase that was positioned directly to the right. I heard people start yelling as if something horrific happened. I sat down on the stairs and began to cry because I didn't know what was going on. My mind was clouded by the screaming, I felt like I had done something wrong because my mother did not return the same desire to be with me as I had for her. She was adamant about getting me to the babysitter, and she came off to my young mind as being very mad. I learned later on that she was heavily influenced by cocaine and alcohol. At that time, I did not know what drugs were, let alone that my mother was on them. I only knew that she appeared mad at me for being home. They finally took me to my babysitter's house, sat me in the living room, and turned on the television set. I was not throwing a fit, but I sat crying uncontrollably in the chair. For some odd reason, I remember Rocky and Bullwinkle were on the television. My babysitter and someone else catty-corner to me were talking about the situation. I have retained the sense of them looking over in my direction as they stood in another room, which was not closed off from the family room. She could have been talking to my mother, but I can't make out who it was. All I remember is the rejection I felt. I literally began repeating over and over again, "My mommy doesn't want me." I might even have been saying it out loud.

At that moment, that situation altered my universe because I had no ability to rationalize what was happening. All I knew was that I wanted my mom, and it felt like I got into trouble for it. Immediately following this, I was sent to live with my father. The transition finalized the rejection I felt, and I would spend the rest of my childhood struggling with rejection and fighting for my mom to be in my life.

2

FOUNDATIONAL YEARS

I believe it was at that moment long ago that the first seed of co-dependency was planted, a co-dependency that was rooted in the fear of rejection. The interpretation of a four-year-old brought about years of confusion and very dysfunctional experiences. It did not take long, of course, to forget that foundational moment upon which my future understanding of relationships was built. The way I viewed the people who cared about me continued to develop even as I lost touch with that moment in time, building layers upon layers of hurt and mistrust on it.

When I moved in with my father, he was not sensitive enough at that particular time in his life to help me process all that was happening. I became emotionally stunted by his actions, which watered the seed of rejection. I began to internalize my feelings, missing out on the truth that my mother did not reject me. She just made a terrible choice, as her addiction ruled her heart. Left to my own thoughts, I started to believe it was my fault she did not want me. This created a belief that no one would ever want me, and before long I believed the lie that something had to be wrong with me.

Throughout my childhood, my mother did not vanish, never

to be seen again. On the contrary, she was around from time to time during holidays and random moments. She became my personal Santa Claus because she always had gifts during her visits. Upon her departure, though, I was often left with more than just a new toy. I usually had another scrape on my scar of rejection.

Lost within the world of her new choices, my mother hurt my mental growth many times over through verbal antics. She doesn't remember the things she did, but that is the thing about intoxication. We do things to others while under the influence. Then when we are sober, we can't even wrap our mind around the awful things we did when confronted by the hurt person. This leaves many dents in the relationship. For the user, it pushes them never to want to leave their rabbit hole. Who likes to face their wrongs, especially when they don't remember doing them? When it comes to the sober loved one, it creates a world of confusion because they are usually driven by their array of emotions concerning the crocodile tears wrapped around reality.

One of the most impactful verbal occurrences was the time she told me that my father never wanted me to be born. I was only five or six years of age. What that did to me deep down was long lasting even in comparison to her thinking it was funny to get me high. The day she told me this was on a visit to the townhouse my father, brother, and I shared in Kendall Lakes, Florida. We had a corner unit that rested against a decent sized lake with a patch of grass against the side of our home. It was there, as we sat on the lawn looking out onto the lake that she told me my father forced her to abort a child, and she had to fight for me to be born. I barely understood what she was telling me, but when she looked at me and boldly said, "Your father did not want you to be born" that cut deep. It was a statement that, although I have healed from it, traumatized me. I would never forget the moment as it played over and over again within my mind during my youth, which only added to my issues with rejection. In the end, it planted a seed of longing for my father's approval. (In my teenage years, I mustered up the nerve to ask my father about that particular statement. He said that he knew immediately that my mother was pregnant with his little girl, denying what she told me. Today, my mother tells me the same story.)

During my childhood, there was a moment in time where I began to shift the sub-conscious blame for my pain and rejection from me to my father. I started to think he was pushing my mother away with his insults. He had a habit of making wise cracks about her, and even to her face. My father never held back his thoughts, and in those moments, I wanted to be her superhero. For a short period of time in my youth, I became her protector against the big bad wolf. I began mouthing off to my father when he said harsh things about her. In my tender heart, I didn't understand the depth of what was going on in the grown-up world. I just wanted my mommy, and I was reaching within my limitations to try and get her. It is kind of like the first time a drug user gets high. Each high afterwards is never like the first, leaving them to chase it through continued and elevated use. My first four years of life were awesome, and I wanted to get back to that contentment. I think that is a normal human reaction, no matter one's age, but I was chasing something that was unrealistic.

Once, on Valentine's Day, the cops showed up. I was across the street at a friend's house. My lack of comprehension concerning the depravity of how my mother was living her life, and the fact that my father was doing his best to protect us from that, flew right over my head. My little friend and I started chanting out the window "Go, mommy, go!" over and over as the cops, my father, and my mom tried to sort out the situation. This is the action of a first grader who was clueless as to how bad that must have been on all sides.

When the cops sent her away, I ran home, and immediately my father yelled for me to go straight to my room. He did not enter my room to talk with me about my wrong behavior. In the heat of his anger, he only knew how to yell, and yelling is putting it lightly. He would go into these very awkward tantrums. At times, things flew, especially his body parts. It made me think that he missed his calling as a dramatic actor. His lack of control always pushed me to shut down, and I would run away to my thoughts and linger in my imagination.

The thing about my imagination was, through circumstances like those, I learned to have a very vivid one. I was a smart little girl. Visual things came easily to me when I applied myself. I only had to watch someone tie his or her shoes a few times to learn on my own. The same was with riding a bike, roller-skating, and all things that took most of the other kids more time to pick up. I remember my brother taking me to learn how to swim, and my stepfather showing me how to skate. They did not have to invest much of their time, though. Not because they didn't want to, but because I caught on quickly. Eventually in my childhood, my imagination became my most nurtured quality.

I spent most of my time alone as a child, so I learned how to be creative. There were even a few times when my imagination made me a little money. My favorite story is the time I put all my stuffed animals in the backyard. I placed each one in a unique place, and charged the kids on the block to visit my "zoo." I advertised through word of mouth, and they came! Then, I reinvested the money in the candy I sold for a profit at school. I was smart, and despite all the craziness, doing things like this brought me great happiness during my childhood.

Overall, as much as I tried, I was never able to reach a place where I felt loved by my mom. The vision of me chasing her down the road when she had to leave must have broken her heart every time. When she did try to explain herself, I could never put two and two together. The feeling of rejection filtered my hearing, and the pain grew into survival skills.

As the road of childhood began to merge into teenage years, after years of feeling neglected, my natural human instinct to protect myself kicked in. I started to see that actions spoke louder than words when it came to people. I didn't want to hold onto false promises year after year anymore, as that was damaging me to do so. By the age of twelve, I stopped believing what people said. I stood by the saying; "Believe nothing of what you hear and half of what you see." However, I never really lost the desire to fight for my mother. The desire may have been expressed through intense anger, but underneath the anger was intense longing. Eventually, that anger became the lens over my scar of rejection, influencing my vision of the world.

ROOTS

We live in a world that says, "You can't teach an old dog new tricks." I believe in a God that says in His Word that He is in the business of renewing the mind.[1] I can testify that He truly is. It took me practically 30 years to finally have those lenses completely broken, so I could truly begin healing and have a healthy outlook of my mother. It happened the day that I realized how forgiven and loved I truly am by God.

You might ask yourself, "What did I have to be forgiven of?" Well . . . my story has only just begun to be told. Just know for now that it was only a couple years after I had already come to faith in Jesus that I was able to forgive my mother entirely. I will never forget my childhood, and the road has been hard balancing forgiveness for her choices and acceptance to how she continues to live her life. She has finally changed how she treats me verbally, especially in the year and a half of writing this story. She has found a path toward repentance and renewal with me. I praise God for every precious moment.

Throughout my journey of healing, God has revealed to me the importance of looking at people through His eyes versus my perception, no matter how spot on I may be. Over time, I have realized that my perception is not always the absolute reality. There are times that something deeper is going on.

Even though my past has taught me a lot about people, it has also filtered my perceptions. Opening my heart and mind to God has taught me to have a teachable spirit, which allows me to have grace for others. Ultimately, it allows me to put into perspective their actions towards me.

I believe God opens our eyes when we take the time to understand where a person has come from without our judgments influencing our opinions. When I look at my mother, I wonder what happened in her life. I don't know much about her childhood or younger years. She has never wanted to share those stories in depth. She always says, "One day, but not yet."

What I do know about her life though is that her alcoholic father abandoned her when she was young, leaving her to be raised by a very strong woman. She was born in Oklahoma and was from my grandmother's second marriage. After my grandparents had been divorced, while my mom was still in her childhood, they moved to Puerto Rico. She grew up there with her half-brother. My mother, if she was anything like me, was a sensitive child in need of tender nurture. The stories

I've heard, however, were that my grandmother was not a very emotionally attentive person. This variance created an unbalanced childhood.

Although my parents were divorced, I got to spend time with my grandmother. My father and my mother's mom were very close, to the point that many people thought she should have been his mother. When my father passed away, we didn't want to tell my grandmother because of how close they were. It was during those years that I got to experience how different my grandmother truly was from my mother.

I heard stories that my grandmother was known to have beat my mother as a child, pushing her to escape to her aunt's house for love and security. My mother loved her aunt so much that I was even named after her. All in all, I really don't know all the details of my mother's life. From what I have been able to discover, my mother has had a lot of pain buried deep down inside. At times, she lets the pain out in front of me, but then she immediately gets angry and bottles it back up. Within the moment, I have tried to show her compassion, but in those moments she has accused me of trying to hurt her. I can only imagine the pain that is there as it has created emotional and mental struggles leaving her with no sense of a safe place to bare it all.

In my grandmother's last days, my mother showed what a caring and beautifully loving daughter she was. She cared for her mother unconditionally and made sure she was never put into an elderly home to wither away. I believe that my mother found solace in caring for a woman who brought her so much pain. What a beautiful picture of restoration and healing.

I never met my grandfather or his family; he died from alcohol poisoning when I was a baby. My mother told me that his family rejected her when she decided to marry my father.

Who knows? Perhaps one day I will meet them and discover their side of the story. My uncle, in recent years, has shared with me about some of my grandfather's American Indian heritage, and I have enjoyed listening. I have Cherokee blood. That is something I am proud of, even though I have yet to meet that side of my family.

My mother told me that my father did not allow her to see her dad on his deathbed. It breaks my heart to think even for one moment that was the case. Supposedly, my father didn't allow my mother to interact with her family in Puerto Rico, either. That does not include her family here in the States. My uncle and his children were very much a part of my life growing up. However, having experienced the dysfunctional drama that exists within her family in Puerto Rico, I would have cut them off, too. There is love within that family, to say the least. But there is also a lot of gossip and hardness toward one another. I, unfortunately, witnessed the behavior created by their perception of reality firsthand, one that is filled with drama towards people they perceive to be doing wrong.

I began to understand the world in which my mother grew up. Emotional abuse that is displayed through mind games is, in my opinion, sometimes worse than being punched in the face. Thus, the thing I took away from that whole experience was that hurting people, when dysfunctional, hurt others to make themselves feel better. I had to realize that truth in order to be able to have forgiveness and compassion for them. I realized this truth again through my healing process because I too have hurt others.

Needless to say, my mother had a very harsh childhood. She never truly received the emotional nurture that she needed to deal with life, and like most people, she forgot the root causes that influenced her toward certain aspects of who she became.

Layer after layer of suffering naturally creates a wall behind which the hurting instinctively defend themselves. This is true especially when one has been severely abused as my mother has. Like many people in her shoes, she has concealed the circumstances, and has learned to shield herself from ever feeling those types of pain again. Unfortunately, marrying someone like my father only deepened her childhood pain. Notwithstanding, I believe if she allows herself to go through the healing process, and forgives others and herself for the choices she has made with her children, the restoration will be ever so beautiful.

3

MY FATHER'S DAUGHTER

The day I went to live with my father and brother, I moved into a one-bedroom apartment. I still have a picture of my father sitting in a chair inside that apartment. He was wearing his typical Polo shirt, shorts, tennis socks, and white sneakers. When I look at the picture now, all I see are his long legs, and I cannot help laughing. He always told me I took after him in that way, but his words were actually, "You take after me, with long legs and a flat chest." There are so many stories about the things my father did. One of the "cleaner" ones was during his bachelor days living in Manhattan. He went to a restaurant wearing his typical garb, and they told him he could not come in unless he was dressed in a tie and jacket. He went home, did not change out of his shorts, but put on a tie and jacket. When he returned, they couldn't deny him entrance.

He was a comedian at heart, so much so that he used to tell jokes on Manhattan street corners back in the 50s. I was told he even had the nerve to go to the Apollo and stand on the stage. I always tell people if you took Frank Sinatra and Mel Brooks and made them one person, that guy was my dad. He may have worn shorts, but he was a sharp looking man, with his diamond pinky ring on his manicured hand, fancy cars, and his many girlfriends. He left his mark on everyone he met. They either loved him or hated him. No matter their opinion, once they met him he was never forgotten.

He was born in the Bronx in 1935, and the youngest of three boys. Those who knew him well never pictured he would end up in suburbia raising two kids on his own. A cousin of mine described him as the "cool uncle who always had a gift in one hand and a hot babe in the other." He was not cut out for the task at hand, especially raising an emotional four-year-old little girl. He was not even suited for a young boy. This was a man who had stacks of porn under his bed, and thought it was funny to hand his 10-year-old little girl a bearded doll asking, "What sex do you think it is?" It was a very awkward moment when I lifted the huge beard, and bam, there was the answer. I would laugh at his perverted jokes, but they always made me uncomfortable. I think it was the strangest for me whenever we went out to eat. It never failed, no matter where we went and no matter what the woman looked like; he would put his arm around the waitress and make me tell her how pretty she was.

There is no mistaking it; a complete and utter "wise guy" raised me. Although he was a self-taught man who became financially successful at a young age, worldly success cannot be equated with wisdom. I am speaking in terms of a bully, a joker, and a man who could manipulate you into buying a wet paper bag. It was the side of him that only those who knew him well got to truly see, but that was who my father was. He was a man who never had a problem confronting people and telling them what he thought. I experienced him doing that on several occasions. I remember the first time I realized I was just like my father in that way. I was thirty years old, and a friend of mine and her son were living in my condo with me. She was dating this guy whom I saw a few days earlier with another friend of mine. I confronted him, and I told him what I thought in such a poetic manner, I had to stop and just relish the moment. It became apparent to me that I was my father's daughter.

All in all, my father truly did the best he knew how to raise his children. I have a lot of crazy and fun memories from growing up with my father, and I cherish every one of them. However, I also spent years in therapy because of it. I never learned as a child how to process my emotions alongside my thoughts because he did not know how to teach me to do so. I had to work through a lot of insecurities and social awkwardness because I too only felt comfortable being an utter and complete wise guy towards people. It took me years to learn the hard way that people do not like that. Further, when my father wasn't yelling, throwing a fit, or hitting me, he was making fun of me similar to a 12-year-old on the playground. Outside of all the goofiness, he had ruined me on the inside, and it took many years with a lot of hard work to understand why I had become so emotionally dysfunctional and ultimately codependent.

A GLIMPSE AT MY FATHER'S PARENTING

My father was a man who did not have healthy relationships with women. He may have been emotional himself, especially in his later years, but handling them was not his strong suit. As he got older, he was involved in all sorts of self-help seminars and 12 step programs. He finally became intimately acquainted with his feelings, but this was after I had left home. When I was still with him, he had difficulty with intimate relationships. He never had a relationship for too long, and when he did, they were chaotic and would affect our household. Women would bang on our front door late at night, and several of his girlfriends pleaded with me, a child, to talk with my father. I never knew how to deal with them, so I would tell them what they wanted to hear.

As a young girl, his inability to communicate with females transferred into our relationship. This was evident in how he dealt with me. For instance, when I cried, I was not comforted. Instead, he would laugh hysterically while calling me names like "Frankenstein." He would keep on with the name calling until I walked away. When I was hurt, I was ignored or sent to my room. When I did something wrong, understandably I was punished, but how he handled it was through ranting and raving. He sometimes tried to reach me through proverbs, such as the time he put on my wall, "When you do good, good things happen, and when you do bad, bad things happen." His actions toward me were contradictory to those written words, and his idea of executing discipline was by charging into my room. I perceived him to be out of control, so I would inevitably find myself shivering in a corner, confused and scared. This chaotic treatment over and over again left me without any mature nurturing toward a healthy way of coping with life.

My father did not finish high school, but he was a self-educated man who surrounded himself with those he could learn from regularly. His outward appearance and success demanded respect from those around him. He had several rules that he lived by, and they were plastered all over our refrigerator. He wanted me to be street smart, so he taught me things like paying attention to the mannerisms of others. He thoroughly enjoyed pointing people out to me. He even instructed me on how to walk down a street so as not to be attacked. That was his Bronx coming out. He would say, "Never count your money in front of other people." He made comments like, "He who has doesn't need to show it." Another saying of his was, "How one keeps his desk is how he keeps his mind." Later in life, I came to learn that statement is not necessarily an absolute truth. A person can appear perfect on the outside, but be tumultuous on the inside.

He succeeded in fooling many people to the point that he got "Father of the Year" once. We were even in the newspaper. He got to tell his story about how hard it was, but what a great job he was doing raising two children on his own. He likened himself to the father in the movie Kramer vs. Kramer. He reveled in having me watch the movie with him, too, so he could point out all the similarities. It always went completely over my head.

Today, when I put things into perspective, he did try hard, and he was doing the best he knew how. I don't necessarily feel sorry for him, though, as a single parent. The reason is simple. When you have the financial means, as he did, it is not as difficult as it is for a person who has to work 9 to 5. He could afford to hire house cleaners to come in, to send his kids to sleepaway camp for eight weeks every summer, and to work from home. I loved him, and I cherish everything he taught me, even when it didn't make sense. All those sayings prepared me for the life I was going to have. Nevertheless, I feel that my youth did not have to be so hard. I can't speak for my brother, as our perceptions of our childhood are different. However, knowing the mental state I have had to overcome only happened through acknowledging the extreme neglect and inconsistency I experienced from my father.

His influence on me was like what any parent would have on their child. That was why at the age of 5, I had already learned the art of manipulation from him. He recorded me trying to con my mother on the phone once. He sat there laughing as he played the recording for me over and over, and then turned to me and said, "Hey kid, you can't con a con artist." He used a more colorful expression, but this was how he was teaching me at the age of five.

Despite some of the characteristics of my dad that I would display from time to time, overall, up to the age of eleven, I was a good kid. I was born healthy, without any medical hindrances, but I still did not learn how to read on a basic kindergarten level until the 3rd grade. My father may have worked for himself, but there was no one home many times when I got there. He never took the time to teach me how to have self-discipline. I don't think my parents even practiced the alphabet with me before I graced the front door of grade school. They were completely self-indulged instead of providing me the care that I needed. For that reason, I was dumped into special learning disability classes (SLD). Those classes had children with real special needs, but there I was, without any real mental problem. All I needed was attention and guidance. It breaks my heart for my young self as I reflect on how I got passed through the system and no one cared to notice me except my third-grade teacher, who I will never forget for as long as I live.

I was attending Kendal Lakes Elementary School, and she was the first person to show me any form of nurture. She saw right through what was happening with me, and she made that year so unforgettable. Unfortunately, though, my father decided we were moving after I had finished the 3rd grade, so just like that, that teacher was taken from my life. Although she had pointed out to him that I just needed some guidance, he still never sat with me or asked if I did my homework, let alone checked if I did. He was too busy with his life, and he preferred introducing me to things that I would crave (such as sushi) as a means of getting me motivated. Overall, he seemed not to care about how well I did.

I failed 6th and 7th grade, but he got me passed through the system somehow. I remained in SLD classes through 8th grade, and could barely read and write by the time I entered high school. Throughout my childhood, there were those like my third-grade teacher who planted seeds of hope in my life, those who allowed me to hope for more for myself. However, the "more" that I wanted was rooted in someone caring about *me*, not my education. In my mind, school was a waste of my time, and I dropped out by the tenth grade. I did get a diploma eventually. At the age of 19, I earned my GED with a score 3 points above passing for each subject. I did not study for the test because I didn't have the discipline to do so. All I knew was that I was very determined not to allow the world that thought so little of me to hold me back.

My father's neglect poisoned my health and wellbeing. His own self-indulgence either had him looking the other way, or he just had some sick means of teaching me life lessons. He never noticed that I bought shoes that didn't fit me. They were always a size too small because I hated having big feet. I ended up with an oversized bone on my left foot by the time I was eighteen. An ATV accident kept my right foot from growing just as large. I still have a scar from that day. As a female growing up solely around guys who were not very sensitive to girls, I especially struggled once I came into my own. I thank God I was at sleepaway camp when I experienced my first menstruation. I don't know what would have happened had I been at home because my father loved embarrassing me. When it came to female necessities, strange women that he randomly knew from his personal life showed up as advisors to me. It was never clear if he was dating them, or if they were just friends or acquaintances. He would just show up at home with them, or take me to their house so that they could talk to me about very personal things. I usually felt so violated by these women whom I didn't even know. He even allowed one of them to move into my bedroom! Although I ended up connecting with her, it was a very humiliating process.

Outside of all the dysfunction, I do remember the joyful times. I also can never deny the American cultural blessings that I had. We went to the Zoo from time to time, and I had birthday parties. My father loved Key West, so we went there many times. Most importantly, I had a roof over my head. My father took me shopping in nice department stores and gave me the freedom to pick out my own style. However, he had a nasty habit of thinking it was acceptable to punish me by taking my clothes away. I was smart, though. I learned quickly to rip off all the tags and wash the garments as soon as I got them.

I played soccer growing up; I played the clarinet, although not well at all. I was a Girl Scout for a few years. I remember the year I ate all the Girl Scout cookies instead of bringing them to the people who bought them. I don't even recall getting into trouble for it because no one ratted on me. While there were so many things that were very wrong about how my father raised me, he also allowed me to partake in plenty of activities that were normal and healthy. Probably the best part of my childhood was that I had a big sister from the Big Brothers and Big Sisters Foundation. Well, I had several of them. I was known for making them leave and not want to return to me. If they got on my nerves, I didn't hold back my thoughts. I made one cry, which often happened when I spoke to other girls as I started to get older. Go figure. I imitated my father. After all, he used to say, "I don't worry about you, kid. You take after me." There were a couple of big sisters whom I adored, and I even did a commercial for the organization. Through Big Brothers and Big Sisters, I got to experience life outside of my home. It was through those experiences that I began to crave something else.

A WALK INTO MY FATHER'S PAST

My father himself was a complex man. I have heard a couple reasons why he wanted to move from New York to Florida. One was that Florida had laws to protect his assets in a divorce, and another was that he wanted to get into real estate investing. Only he knows which of the two are true, if not both, but I believe he always wanted to get away from his family. It must have been much harder for my brother to make that move because he spent the first six years of his life around family. I don't remember much about my grandparents, and my father was in and out of a relationship with his brothers. Therefore, my brother and I were kept isolated from our family to a certain extent by living in Florida. I remember talking to my grandparents on the phone from time to time. My grandmother would complain about her aches. We did know one uncle and his children who were already grown by the time I was born. This uncle came to Florida to visit yearly, and I absolutely adored him. I always looked forward to seeing him when he visited.

The first ten years of my father's life were spent experiencing the Great Depression and hearing of the Holocaust as a Jewish boy of German and French descent. Outside of a mother who emotionally damaged my father, these two events influenced him deeply. As a result of the Great Depression, we always had an abundance of products in our home such as canned foods and other necessities.

We were not religious in practice, but my father went out of his way to instill pride in our Jewish heritage. I remember when we first moved from Long Island to Kendall Lakes, Florida. At that time, Kendall was a rather rural area. There were strawberry fields, cornfields, and cow pastures all over. My father, brother and I eventually moved to a townhouse in a neighborhood called Lake Laura. I have many memories of living there. One of them is the family next door that would consistently call us derogatory names. I suppose they didn't like Jewish people very much. My father would not allow us to respond. He would say, "Keep your head up and be proud of who you are." I know he confronted them a few times, but I don't remember my father wasting too much of his energy on them. In Lake Laura, we weren't the only Jewish family, but it was there that I thought I learned how Gentiles saw Jewish people. I was subjected to awful things being said by other kids. When we moved to Cooper City three years later, I met a young blonde girl that came from a very conservative Christian home. I remember her sharing that, in her faith, she wasn't allowed to cut her hair, and she could only wear dresses. I found her very fascinating. Sadly, she also would tell me things like, "Jews killed Christ so you are a Christ killer," and "You are the seed of the devil." I showed her my tailbone and said, "Look, this is where they cut the tail off." Needless to say, my father ingrained in me a love for our heritage and ability to stand up for myself with a hint of humor.

It is no exaggeration that my grandmother's abuse of my father had a more lasting impact on him than the Great Depression, and the Holocaust combined. Out of respect for my family, I will hold back some of the more gruesome details. However, the dysfunction that developed in his childhood was rooted in his inability to know that his mother loved him. All his issues are summed up in a story about him at the age of three. I have a picture of him dressed as a little girl. In the Jewish culture, we don't cut a child's hair until they reach the age of three. The story is told that my grandmother wanted a little girl, and my father had to bear the brunt of that not happening. She put the boy into a beauty contest, and he won! I can't tell you how many times when I was just a child myself, I would have to listen to him cry over how his mother never loved him. He even had a recording of her talking, and he would constantly say to me, "Listen, listen, she won't say she loves me." The sad part is, over the past few years, I have gotten to know my uncle who my father spent most of his life estranged from. This uncle was the middle child, and he told me how my grandmother loved my father very much. I have also learned that my grandmother had many issues that impacted the two younger boys. Learning these things have helped me understand that, like myself, my father never gained the healthy nurture he needed to deal with life, thus living out the cycle of abuse and neglect from one generation to the next.

AN OLDER BROTHER

My father's upbringing accounts for much of my childhood experiences, but my brother had a very different experience growing up. My father and brother seemed to me like distant beings when I was growing up with them. I did not have the social skill set my big brother did. It is no secret that we were given very different platforms to stand on; for example, while my brother had a typical high school life with friends and social involvement, I barely made it to ninth grade and dropped out by tenth. He also got along with my father better than I did, or I should say, he had a more stable approach to do so. From a younger sister's point of view, he had my father's affection and an easier road than me.

I looked up to my brother and admired him so much. When we did engage with each other, he was a typical big brother to me. We wrestled, and he locked me into closed spaces; we yelled at each other, he chased me with his boogers, and my constant following always bothered him. In my worldview tainted by rejection, though, all I saw was a big brother whom everyone liked (more than me); my perception was clouded by his lack of desire to be close to me in a real and nurturing way. I had also created a Brady Bunch expectation of what a brother should be by comparing how I saw my friends' big brothers engage with them. I declared in my mind that there was something wrong with me since my brother did not treat me the same way. This fed my insecurities and turned up the flame that screamed, "no one wants me."

In our home life, I spent most of the time in my room due to being in trouble for one reason or another. I would sit on my dresser, staring out the window, dreaming of a better life. When it came to getting scolded, my brother got into trouble too, but I seemed to get into trouble for most of the incidents that happened in our home. I remember one occasion in particular. All the towels went missing, and my brother's room looked like a bomb had exploded. The smell was even similar to a sewer. My room, which was spotless and organized, had no trace of them. Yet, I spent the weekend punished due to the disappearance of the towels. Maybe my father thought I had burned them or given them away. Who knows? Instead of getting to the bottom of the situation, it was easier for my father to keep me trapped in my room. That particular situation got worse as my brother, and several of the neighborhood kids taunted me outside my window. I got so mad that I kicked it, and it did exactly what windows do when you kick them. It shattered, and that led to a longer punishment, of course.

I am sure if you asked my brother, he feels the same way I do, that he had it harder than me. We always feel like our treatment was worse than our siblings, but ultimately I felt like the scapegoat that was released into the wilderness to die by my family.

I have developed a lot of compassion for my brother over the years. I know the divorce had to have been hard on him, and my mother did things to him that I saw were hurtful. The memory that stands out was when she showed up drunk at his Bar Mitzvah. That must have been the day he realized many things about his mom. I try to put myself into his shoes. He had the first seven years of his life rooted in a home with a father and mother. I have never talked to him about what life was like for him back then, or how he felt through the transition of the divorce. I could only imagine, though, how his life turned upside down when it happened. Then to be humiliated during a very special day must have reopened the wound that was already present within his young heart. With a shattered reality and the lack of stable parents, my brother could not, in a healthy way, process what was going on. I believe my brother, in his own way, created a survival mode for himself gleaning from the only influence he had: my father.

Eventually, I ran away from home at the age of fourteen, creating a wider gap between my brother and myself. I must have hurt him deeply by my actions, even though we were not the best of friends. The thing was, from an outside perspective, he had a better skill set within the circumstance he found himself. He knew how to plug into healthier outlets than I did. Personally, I was utterly lost within my mind and trapped by my emotions. In truth, I can only speculate concerning my brother. When I look back and study our dynamics, I can see how he probably saw me as a weird sister who he could not connect with at all. He had no idea what I was struggling through, so from the outside I appeared to have just flipped out emotionally at the age of fourteen, leaving him to ride the crazy train, known as our family, alone. Ultimately, our lives split for many years, because he went to college, and I went straight to surviving the streets of Ft. Lauderdale.

The things that happened in my childhood took their place in the lies that would control my perception of who I was and the world around me. These lies would haunt my thoughts as I tried to grow up. I believed, deeply, all the lies about myself that were based on the things that had happened to me. The good, the bad, and the ugly all filled my mindset of who I was. I walked away from my younger years angry because those I loved most appeared not to like me due to rejection and neglect. I was determined to learn on my own how to survive this life, and find people who would want me. I can still see myself when I left with a little bag on my shoulder, and my father standing in the driveway. I turned back and yelled, "I will do this on my own even if it is the hard way." "On my own" and "the hard way" is what I got. There were plenty of children who had similar and/or worse circumstances than I did, and my journey was about to connect me to them. Together we would seek to conquer the world.

4

STATE OF CONFUSION

....

The song by Bon Jovi, "Runaway" plays over and over again in my mind as I begin to reflect over the next period of my life. That song was my anthem back in those days, as it spoke about me; I was the girl described in that song to some degree. I clutched at those words from my teenage years, when I ran away from my father's house, until I was older. Had it been possible, the song would have burnt itself into my Sony Walkman and played without a cassette (That's right, I just mentioned the Sony Walkman. Oh, how I loved the 80s).

When I was a young girl, music helped me escape from the world around me. The lyrics of songs helped me develop a tremendous imagination. I found myself often creating many different fantasy worlds. If only I had known to pen them. Overall, I believe that music encouraged me and taught me how to seek beyond my circumstances. I would cling to lyrics and make them my own. I always found an inclination toward strong women who sung about fighting to survive in a world that tried to hold them back. The stories in those songs helped me to know that I was not alone, and in them I found comfort.

A FORWARD PAUSE

As the 80s moved on, the dark path that was about to become my past was beckoning me. There was no doubt that I heard it calling, because I ran hard and fast toward it, and eventually down it. The harshness of my youth became very clear to me at 32 years old. Therefore, before I continue telling my story, I would like to bring you into that future setting. I had moved to North Carolina that year. This was one year after accepting that Jesus is my Messiah. I had a strong desire to move away from South Florida at that point in my life, and a friend at the time wanted to take off with me. He convinced me to buy a house there with him and his sister instead of just renting. At this time, I was still very much putting my confidence in my human relationships. This is why I agreed, because I thought they truly cared about investing in a future together. I believed they were going to move there with me, but they never showed. Well, she did, but that lasted only a couple months. I was left with so much responsibility on my hands, but that situation was used to teach me so much about myself. In the midst of it, though, it was just another drop in the bucket compared to what I had experienced in my past.

I found myself in this house, alone in a foreign state without a single friend. As I was sitting there night after night by myself, I contemplated, "What just happened the first 32 years of my life?" If you can picture in your mind the look of a cat's face when you throw it into the water and it scrambles out as fast as it can, that was how I felt.

As I genuinely began unpacking my life, I was truly in shock. I began to enter into a deep depression that would last for the following six years. I did a great job of hiding it while I was living in North Carolina, but only because no one truly noticed me there. Only a select few did, and I thank God for each and every one of them, primarily, for my spiritual mother and father. They found me in a new members' class at church, and came alongside me. It must have been a mother's instinct considering how well I hid my emotions overall. I believe it was because I had come out of the depths of utter darkness, and despite my depression, there was a burning within, a pure hunger to know God. I had the willingness to do the work it was going to take to figure out my mess. It was through that journey that I have been able to revisit every aspect of my past. It excites me to know that I am now able to share openly about the dark path I went down.

A Backward Pause

I want to share one more reflection, but this time it is a glimpse into my childhood. Prior to running away from my father, something happened that altered me. It was as if I had been pushed to my limit, and at twelve years of age, I snapped. A fire was kindled within me, and the flames began to grow. It was 1985-86, and my first year in middle school. My father and my mother were getting along for the most part, and he was allowing us to visit her. She began to pull herself together after a really bad scare that landed her in jail. She almost killed a family while driving drunk, and she was put into the Care Unit, a rehab center for addicts. When she got out, she and her husband moved to Bradenton, Florida. They used the AA program in the center, and it was there she learned that you have to remove yourself from people, places, and things in order to get a clear focus on life. This is from an addiction perspective, and a choice that really does make a difference when you need to get your head straight. It doesn't apply if you are just running away from a hard situation. However, my mother followed the advice, and they picked up and moved from South Miami to Bradenton. It was there she decided to go to nursing school, and by the grace of God she was able to get her charges dropped. My father even paid for her tuition, or at least helped her. Things were off to a fresh start. She even bought a house, and I was excited. This specific year, I was going to spend Christmas vacation with her.

At that time we lived in Cooper City, so my parents would meet in Naples, Florida. It was a perfect halfway point between Bradenton and our new house. The long journey going down "Alligator Alley" was daunting and scary. In those days, there was nothing on either side of the one-way highway but sawgrass, water, and gators. I think it was during those trips I learned to talk with God because I would silently pray for the trip the whole way. Once we arrived, the exchange was always awkward, but we got through it. This particular year, my cousins came to visit, and the house was filled with so much fun. I even made a new friend across the street from her house. This little girl lived in a tree house, and I thought it was the neatest place on earth.

One of my favorite childhood memories comes from that visit. My brother always thought it hilarious to pass gas on my mother and me. I will never forget thinking how cool my mom was as she woke me up in the middle of the night just so we could get my brother back as a team. It took us a while to plot something that we both loved, but I think that we came up with the greatest plan ever. We stood over him while he slept and giggled over how we were going to tell him that we passed gas on him while he was asleep. Not only that, but, as he smelt it he smiled sniffing the air! It was not until a few years ago that he learned the truth. That visit was the one and only time it actually felt like a family, and things were great. I couldn't have asked for anything more, except for one thing that seemed so simple to my mind. That was, I was hoping it was finally going to happen. I was going to get my mom back. I built up the courage to ask her if I could move in. Her answer was no.

We sat in a doorway towards the back of the house that led to a spare guest room that was added on. They had some guy renting it at the time. It was her and her husband, and they so kindly explained to me why it was not feasible. Looking back, I can see them really caring. They were so attentive to my feelings, but sadly, all I could hear was a rejection. It was as if by the age of 11, after so much heartache, I couldn't handle "no." Something inside me changed. I began to feel angry, and that feeling began to spread throughout my whole being. It did not help that after they refused me, my mother pulled me to the side and scared me with her words. She informed me that I should tell her if my stepfather or their male friend that lived with them ever did anything sexually inappropriate to me, thus planting fear and distrust within me. I was used to men being perverted around me because of my father, but up to this point I had always felt safe around my stepfather. He was always laid back, silly, and told funny jokes. For the rest of the visit I managed to hold it together externally, but when I returned home I was not the same child my father dropped off.

The transition from a somewhat respectful child to a flippant and disrespectful child began, and by my twelfth birthday I was acting out everywhere. I would cause trouble at school, and when my teachers would tell me to stop, I would stand on the table and tell them to make me. I got kicked out of sleepaway camp, and I began to sneak out of my bedroom window. We lived in a two-story house, but I became skilled at climbing the walls of that place. The longing that began to build inside of my heart to find people who I could connect with outweighed my fear of heights. A sense of entitlement started to develop. If I wanted something, I took it. I even had the nerve to steal from my little girlfriends. I would ask to borrow their gold, and never return it, unless they went out of their way to ask for it. It was also at this time that I started fighting with people. I went from an introvert to an extrovert when it came to dealing with people.

I became friends with a troubled girl who "slept around." I did not follow in her footsteps in that regard; I maintained at least that level of innocence. I just really enjoyed being around her. My creepy father really liked her too, and he allowed me to be friends with her. However, I loved disobeying my father at this stage. I was not going to allow him to keep me trapped in my room any longer. I was going to take whatever I wanted from this world, because I knew it wasn't going to give to me on its own. I just ceased caring about the consequences. My father took notice, and he began looking for some solutions. One was a private Yeshiva that had opened up in my neighborhood. The mere sight of all the Orthodox kids terrified me, and I pleaded for my life and freedom.

Perhaps his breaking point was the night I sneaked out against his wishes because my neighbor was having a party at the local arcade. My father showed up there with a large paddle and began screaming at me in public. I ran as fast as I could to get home before he did, and kept my door locked for the rest of the night. This all ended with a huge fight in which he realized the only solution was to give me what I always wanted: to go live with my mother. It happened within days, and by this time, she was almost finished with her nursing degree. However, she had sold her nice house and was living in a small apartment.

The day I left, I refused to talk to my father the whole ride to the airport. He had a friend of his fly me in his single engine to where my mother was living. All I remember is the hate I felt towards him as he stood on the roadway right outside of the airplane's window. In my mind, he just didn't care about me. He only cared about himself because he never tried to invest in my life. Odds are, though, if he had the ability to look into the future, he would have cared enough to not send me into what was in store for me. I had become a terror to be reckoned with and he was sending me to two people who were set in their ways. They most certainly did not know how to deal with me.

I chuckle at my young self now; I thought I was a hardcore little girl. Twisted Sister's "We're Not Gonna Take It" expressed my emotions, thought process, and attitude toward authority. It only took a month at my new school for trouble to find me. A gang of African American girls decided they did not like me, and they tried messing with me. For weeks, they mouthed off at me, and eventually they followed me home. I was already street smart, though. I knew that they were following me, so I took off all my gold chains. Yes, I said "all." The 80s were a cruel time in fashion, and I loved wearing 5 to 6 chains at one time. I stashed my books and gold in a bush. I then proceeded to wait for them. I gathered it was better to face them than to run and have to deal with it in the future. They eventually showed up, and there we were gathered out on a main road. I remember there was a 7-Eleven just a block away, and we stood on a patch of grass adjacent to where I lived. They commissioned their little white friend to fight me one on one, but I took her out. I already had so much pent-up anger, so I just unleashed it. Plus, I had an older brother who wrestled with me all the time. She was not a threat to me. Next thing I remember, two or three of them came after me, and I did the best I could to hold my own.

That was my first of many fights, and I wasn't even

phased by it. That situation oddly opened things up for me at that school. I had earned respect, I suppose. One of the girls approached me a few days later. She told me how she had heard I had a rough life, and that was why I was now living in her town. She actually apologized, but I told her "whatever" and walked away. I just did not care. Although deep down inside I longed to be accepted, I had lost my faith in people. I did allow myself to make a few friends. Just like the statement "Misery loves company," I say, "Trouble finds trouble." Though one of them was really sweet, the other two girls were on the same path as me. I connected with one of them so well; it was like we were two lost sisters who found each other. I got my hair cut into this shaved short hairstyle like hers, and we even wore similar outfits. She introduced me to my first experience with drugs. I began to pop speed on my way to school, and afterwards we just looked for whatever trouble we could find. We would go and peek into the local strip club, and then run away laughing.

Although I remember well all three of the girls I hung with, I will never forget this one. She and I met up walking about in the area we lived. We both lived in apartment complexes that were surrounded by trees and cow fields. I remember the cow fields because one day my mother, stepfather, and I were driving home from dinner. I got into a big argument with my stepdad. I don't even remember what it was about, but I jumped out of the car. My mother followed me, and he took off. The best route for us to walk home was through a cow pasture. We jumped the fence and cut through, which was fine until we realized there was a bull coming right towards us! My mental image of the situation is priceless. We began to run for our lives, and when we got back to our apartment complex my stepdad was casually swimming in the pool! My mother and I were laughing and yelling at him. We didn't know if we should be mad or happy. What a memory!

This particular girlfriend was my first real friend. She "got" me, and we proceeded to do stupid things together. We wanted to do something we could always remember each other by. So after about 6-8 months of living with my mother, we decided to mark our skin with a hot cigarette lighter, and I still have the scar on my arm. Unfortunately, when my mother saw the mark, she was convinced that I wanted to hurt myself. That led her to put me into a rehabilitation center. However, before that happened, I had a lot of freedom living with her and a lot of time on my hands to find trouble. I don't recollect her or my stepfather being home often. I used to sit around in the apartment smoking their cigarettes and listening to the Beastie Boys. I did not care that they were not home. I wasn't locked away in a castle, and I was able to roam around as I pleased. Of course, this was to my detriment.

Once, my girlfriend and I met some older boys that we flirted with. I ran my mouth to one of them, and it cost me my virginity. This eighteen-year-old boy raped me, a little twelve-year-old girl. Only two of my girlfriends knew, and they were extremely concerned for me. They kept trying to get me to tell someone, but I wouldn't. I just blamed myself. It was only a week later that my mother and stepfather found me, out and about, and they forced me into their car. When they got me into the car I was screaming and fighting with such fervor that a cop pulled us over on our way to the children's correctional center.

I think my mother did the right thing putting me into that center. It all boiled down to two things: the burn on my arm, and what I did the day after I was raped. My mother had a friend over, and although I don't remember what caused me to be upset at her, I pulled a knife on her. We can all agree that I was out of control.

I don't remember the actual name of the facility I went to, but I do remember what we called it on the inside: Palm's Prison. It was a place for psychologically troubled kids. I did not want to be there, but I retained the memories from my time there like it happened yesterday. There were actually rooms there that had padded walls. I never had to go into one, thankfully, and I eventually convinced my father to get me out. He became my hero for doing so, too. However, it is a shame that he did. I believe, had he left me there, I might have avoided many of the horrible choices I was about to make that led to many more hardships.

5

LEAVING HOME

It was the summer before I moved out of my father's house when I met the girl who became the doorway to my teenage havoc. She was this really fun and silly girl who was exceptionally pretty. Her mother was a photographer, and their whole garage had been converted into a studio. The first time I went to her home, she gave me the grand tour of all her modeling pictures. Having been a tomboy and somewhat awkward, I did not know how to relate whatsoever. In my home, I didn't have a mother that pampered me like that. I had a father who had no idea how to raise a little girl.

Like many little girls though, I remember the first time I even thought about wanting to be "pretty looking." There came that point in my young life where I noticed the difference between myself and other girls, and I found myself drawing inspiration from my neighbor. The thing was, she looked like Barbie and I looked like Ken, the brunette version. She had a full head of hair that was long, blonde, and straight compared to my dry, curly, and short hair. My inspiration ran deep, as I begged my dad one day to take me to the hairdresser to get it straightened. What can I say? I was ambitious. When we got there, the stylist actually ended up perming my already curly hair. Instead of newly beautiful, I looked like I had gotten into a fight with a poodle. In addition, as tan as I was, I ended up looking like the little Spanish boy my father always wanted.

All that to say, I was in awe that my new friend wanted to take me under her wings, like a little sister. I could not get enough of her constructive criticism. A whole world opened up to me, and I began to learn about things like clothes and makeup. As she sat me down to teach me the art of wearing makeup, she didn't teach me "less is more". She taught me to paint my face, and I became an imitation Picasso. The canvas of my face looked like a cross between King Tut with my eyeliner, and a clown with bright red lipstick and blush. Thank God my father was dating a lady who owned a salon at the time. She and I convinced him to allow me to go get pampered in order to learn rightly how to wear makeup. He eventually agreed, and I had my first makeover where I learned how to lightly apply cosmetics. It was great.

That same day I spent the night at my girlfriend's house, and it was that evening that my life changed forever. My friend was so excited when I got to her house. She wanted to take me to this "cool place," so I agreed. It was called Nepenthe, a Fort Lauderdale nightclub for teenagers. At the age of thirteen almost fourteen, I walked into this place, and felt like I was walking into a movie. It was dark with flashing lights, and the air had a fog to it. Music was playing, and there were kids running around. I instantly fell in love. It even served punch and soda for free with a hot bar filled with food. (I don't think people actually ate that food. At least I hope not!) It had some of the greatest freestyle concerts by popular artists of the day, such as "Freestyle". I can still hear the song "Don't Stop The Rock" in my mind as I picture the scene. I felt free when we were there, and it seemed as if all my cares slipped away. This place also attracted kids from Miami, and it was that first night I met a young man who I developed a deep crush for. I also met two of my dearest friends, Antoinette and Nickie. They were sitting on a speaker, and I thought they were the most fantastic girls I had ever met from the moment we greeted one another. I had no idea the things we would endure together, and that they would become my friends for life.

Contemplating my first teenage crush, which lasted for what seemed like a lifetime, brings a chuckle and a "What were you thinking?" He was part of a larger body of young men we coined "Nicas." That was short for Nicaraguan. These Miami Latin boys we met at this club, with their Cavaricci pants and buttoned down shirts left slightly open, looked like the Italian guy from Brooklyn with all his gold chains screaming down the street, "Hey, Vinnie!" Instead they were screaming, "¡Ojo! Que Ola?" with some colorful expletives. They were all illegally in the U.S., and I was blinded by how much fun it was to hang out with them. The thing about having male friends prior to that was, I only had your typical middle school boyfriend experiences. That's right, not much experience. Those are the years everyone just starts "exploring." I dated a couple different boys, but each one of them broke up with me within a few weeks. That never bothered me. I knew that middle school boys were within their explorative years. I had an older brother, so I understood this. I, on the other hand, was far from explorative, and lost everything the one time I flirted with a boy. Kids can be curious with one another, playing silly games, but when a child becomes too confident in their curiosity, it usually ends with a bad result. Typically, my big mouth would make boys think things that I truly would never want to happen. For instance, there was this particular boyfriend that dated me simply because I "ran my trap." In reality, I would run away as soon as I saw him. I would get so scared he would want to kiss me. When school would let out, I would escape to my bus as fast as I could, hoping he would not see me. I was secretly terrified of that kiss.

My crush, however, is another story. The memories flow like a river as I begin thinking about the night I met him at Nepenthe. Those thoughts also make me reflect on my first year of seminary. It was in my Introduction to Biblical Counseling class that the professor began teaching how to tell when you enter into an unhealthy relationship. He began singing "I can't live, if living is without you," and then proceeded to say, "If someone sings that to you, RUN!"

That sums up my very first crush experience, and yes, at thirteen I was the one singing that song. He turned on what I call his, "Latin charm." As a little girl who had a broken heart from her family, it was easy for me to fall for his lyrics. He must have read romance novels because he spoke empty, but sweet, words to me. The night we met, we escaped to a corner and I experienced my first consensual kiss. Who knows if he even told me his real name? All I knew was that I liked him, and I wanted to be around him.

The longing to be loved and wanted by him consumed my thinking for months. He would visit me while I was still living with my father. Then, like any boy with wrong intentions, he visited me after dark. In what I thought was love, I did not care as long as he was there. Not surprisingly, he ended our relationship not long after it began, as a kiss was all he would get. I did not want to believe that I was prone to rejection, so I suppressed those feelings of devastation. It was easy to suppress my emotions; after all, that was how I was taught to deal with my feelings. I think the only time I really expressed my emotions was when my girlfriends and I would ridiculously sing all the freestyle love songs together, while thinking about our Latin boyfriends. The lyrics of those songs did not help my dysfunctional attachment towards wanting to be loved and accepted. They only fed the fire.

THE MOVE

It was 1988, and my brother had graduated high school and left for college as I entered ninth grade. This transition was a few months after my breakup, and as I entered this foreign place called "high school," I looked around to find no familiar faces. Most of my friends from middle school now lived within a different district, and I found myself under the shadow of my big brother, something I could not live up to even if I tried. A mere couple of months into my ninth grade year, I realized that I was in a world in which I did not fit. I was emotionally and mentally light years away, and I could not find a platform to ground myself on. At the time I could not fathom the amount of self-awareness it takes to make changes in one's life. There must be a certain openness to the discomfort that pumps through a body, there must be a yearning for change. At fourteen, I operated out of my pain that was swimming within me, so I packed my bags and left as fast as I could.

My father and I got into a major fight the day I left, but I can't recall the details. I do remember yelling at him that he would no longer abuse me as I ran from him down the street. I ended up calling some people I had met through my crush, and they came and picked me up. I stayed with them in this apartment that was basically a funnel of people all day and night. I lived with them for several months, until my mother decided to pack her things up, and move back to the East Coast near me. I was almost fifteen by the time she arrived.

She silently gave up a lot to move back to the area that once drew her into addiction. She had finally established roots as a nurse. She had met some really special friends that she was investing in. She chose me, though. She put me above all that she had, and although she was never going to be the mother that I needed or wanted emotionally, that action spoke very loudly of her love for me.

However, in my blindness I could not comprehend, let alone appreciate, her actions at the time. Instead, I badly mistreated her once we were together because I was lost in my anger. I had become a cruel young woman, and although they were drug users, they were trying the best they knew how.

We now lived in a town called Coconut Creek. My new high school was a bit on the rough side compared to Cooper City, where I lived previously. Cooper City High School was predominately white, and only had about 500 students at the time, all from middle to upper class families. They had their issues, but it was a daisy group of kids compared to my new school. At Coconut Creek it was perfectly mixed, and I found the troubled kids as fast as a pig finds a fresh mud-hole. I think I went to class about 10 times the whole semester I was there. The beach, my apartment, and any wormhole had more attraction for me than school. I was already a drug user, and due to my first crush, I found an affinity towards the Latin and African American kids. I spent my weeks doing drugs and "chilling", and on the weekends my Miami guy friends would pick me up to go club hopping. It was easy to sneak into clubs back then because they were 18 and older, so as long as we didn't drink within the club, we were fine.

After ninth grade had ended, I convinced my mother to move to a town called Sunrise, so I could be close to my friend from sleepaway camp. That summer we moved, and my camp friend introduced me to the girls who became my family. There were many girls, who will not be mentioned by name, in our tight knit group, and we just got one another. There were those of us who came from broken homes, and others who just came from dysfunctional foundations. A few had solid roots within their nuclear families, but happened to be attracted to the life of the rebellious. The two I met at the club, Nickie and Antoinette, were among these girls. These two, along with several others, really impacted my life the most. I found myself within a group of girls who all had strong minds, strong wills, and the ability to get what they wanted. To sum it up, we partied like rock stars. I already knew how to speak my mind, and I was already strong willed, but it was through them that I learned survival skills. Most importantly, on a journey in a world that did not care about me, I found my companions.

6

REBELLION

It was after my mother and I moved to the city of Sunrise, Florida that my life began to sink deeper. Exactly how it happened is tucked deep within my subconscious memory. All I know is that outside of my girlfriends, I found comfort in the gang world. I became very close to the members of Zulu in my local area. There were a couple of chapters at the time in South Florida. One of the seasoned members of a specific chapter nearby became like a big brother to me. He had recently gotten out of jail, and his ex-girlfriend had gone back to her home country. We were able to talk and confide in each other about our lives. I would hang out with him at his family's house, and he treated me with, what I perceived to be, such respect. It was the first time in my life that I felt special.

The thing about gangs is they are territorial, even with one another. It should be to no surprise that my actions were watched very closely. Hanging out with a non-member guy was an act of cheating, and when I did, such as the day I was with a close friend of mine, they jumped the poor kid. It was awful. I helped him into his car as quickly as I could, and I went looking for the members. Luckily, I found them in a gas station parking lot, and I ran towards them, yelling like a banshee. I almost got slapped around for causing a scene, but instead, we all made our way to my friend's house. To their surprise, he forced them to their knees to apologize.

During the days that I hung out with these guys, my mother and stepfather would vanish for what seemed like weeks at a time. When they were gone, we would hold gang membership fights at the complex because there was a large field in the back. The funniest memory was that my stepfather refused to purchase living room furniture for a long time because of the crowd I was bringing into the apartment. It was crazy; they would graffiti the walls of the entrance every time the walls were cleaned up with fresh paint. We would have what we called, "stoner parties." All my girlfriends would come over, and we would cook up a storm. We were living life with no authority, and no fear of getting into trouble. We were out of control, and I would have to beg the owners of the complex many times to not evict my mother. To add to the situation, I would often come home smashed out of my skull, and my mother and stepfather would be cracked out themselves. We would sit around together, all high as kites.

Living with my mother and stepfather, although they tried to be a part of my life, was virtually living on my own. She attempted to discipline me at times, but I would laugh at her and walk out. I had become a very nasty girl in attitude and behavior. Our relationship, when we were sober around each other, was horrific. I needed to be locked up, and I am surprised that my anger never pushed me to kill anyone, including myself. The number of holes my stepfather had to patch in our walls and the way I would swing at others was shocking. I even had the audacity to hit my mother, and the fact that I did brings me to tears. The remorse is indescribable. I brought my violence to the streets, too, and I was ready to fight anyone who wanted to "throw down." I even fought a couple of my girlfriends, Nickie included. I didn't care. That was how I dealt with life, through violence. Violence is most likely what drew me into the world of a gang.

My rebellion bled into every corner of life. For instance, there were countless times my friends and I lied to boys so we could borrow their cars and money. The thing was, we didn't even have drivers' licenses, and we were not old enough to drive without supervision. There were times we even hitchhiked, and would con the driver to pay our way into a club or to buy us food. The foolishness that ran within our thinking is exemplified in a specific story.

Two friends of mine and I manipulated some kid we were so called friends with into lending us his car. We hitched a ride down to his job, and next thing we knew we were driving off with his car. We were only supposed to go down the street because he was at work, and anything more was not part of the deal. Well, we decided we were going to visit Miami instead, so we began driving (or I should say crawling) down the street. It was a stick shift, and we had no clue how to drive one. It was dark out by the time we got to Miami. I was in the back seat, with my two friends in the front. All of a sudden the one in the passenger seat looked over and said, "Do you notice all the cars are honking at us?" The one driving replied, "That is because they see how pretty we are." I calmly responded, "No, we are driving the wrong way." We made a turn as soon as we could, and once through the intersection, there was not enough time to stop laughing as we got pulled over. The cop said, "Do you realize all we saw is a little white car putting through the intersection with no lights on?" A long story short, they had the car towed, and hauled our butts to jail. Fortunately for us, they did not book us. We sat in the lobby of the station, and my mom was the parent who came to get us.

Despite the trouble we got into, we learned how to get whatever we wanted. We each had different skills we brought to the table, and some of us had better manipulation skills than others. Overall, we made a great team. We were not just some spoiled kids trying different things; we were young girls whose parents didn't pay much attention to us. In reality, though, had our parents given us the right nurturing, we would have been good girls. As creative and full of life as we were, with the right motivation, we would have done great things with all that energy. However, we were only working with what we had —manipulation and a desire to survive in a world that taught us to be tough and thick-skinned. There was nothing that was going to hold us back. I could write a book solely about the adventures we had. The stories are unreal, and writers could not even make up half of what we did. I know with all my heart that God was watching over us because we could have been kidnapped, raped, murdered, and the Lord only knows what else He protected us girls from. For the harsh reality was that we were relentless and had no fear of anyone or anything.

OFFICIALLY ON MY OWN AT SIXTEEN

It did not even take a year of living in Sunrise before Nickie and I worked it out for us to move in with one of her sisters. She was the youngest of a large family, and we moved in with the second to youngest of the girls. My father paid my rent, surprisingly. The terms were that I got a part time job, and kept it while attending classes. I got a position working at the mall at a spy shop. I liked it. Believe it or not, I actually attended my classes, too. It took a lot of convincing for the school to even allow us to be there. Due to the fact it was a prestigious high school, they did not want us to enroll, as we were not "living at home." It also didn't help that my transcript screamed, "troubled." I realized that I had to play my cards right. It was no longer just about me and my future, but also Nickie's and she was my dearest friend. She was not only the prettiest girl I had ever met, but she was also hilarious, and she always had a plan. She tried many times to help me find confidence in myself, but she was never able to reach me in a way that brought healing. That was only something God was going to do. At that point, bitterness had taken root within my heart, and it continued to grow day by day.

During our time as roommates, I intentionally attempted to focus on school, something I had never really done before. I was in a really good educational institution for the first time, and some of my old sleepaway camp acquaintances attended it as well. My time there was not without some positive influences. For instance, I discovered that I loved art class, and remember having a picture of crazy lines put on display at a fair. It felt good, and was the first time I felt accomplished. I was embarrassed to tell anyone about my artwork, but I still got my crew to go to the fair. Once we were there, I snuck away to go see it by myself. I think Nickie may have known, but no one else noticed. As for the two of us, we were not typical high school students, and together, we really stood out. Nickie had a lot to do with that. She was ahead of her time when it came to fashion. She designed outfits and hair styles that people were not ready to embrace. Today, I turn on the TV and most women I see on reality TV shows are dressed in the style she paraded back then. I remember going to the mall with her to acquire those outfits, thinking we had the right to take whatever we wanted. It was only by the grace of God that we never got caught. We would frequently steal clothes from large department stores, and then turn around and return them for money. It was such a gambit we had going on. Our skills were developed; I remember Nickie snatching a large human like doll right in front of a cashier. That lady had no idea what was happening right in front of her!

Overall, those days with Nickie still have a sweet place in my heart. We had many good times outside of our troubles and bad choices. One of my best memories is the two of us laughing the whole way to school as we rode the bus. Our laughter was basically due to the fact we lived on our own, but had to ride on a school bus. Nickie, unlike myself, was a very determined young girl who knew what she wanted out of life. She actually excelled at that high school, and graduated playing her cards right. While I, on the other hand, decided it was an excellent idea to move to Miami with my trashy boyfriend. She tried to stop me, but I was convinced that it was my only option. It was through that choice though that I lost the last of my innocence.

7

MARRIAGE AND
A FATHER'S TOUGH LOVE

....

While I was still living with my mother, right before I moved in with Nickie, I began dating the boy who would become my husband. I was sixteen by this time, and he caught my attention one day while I was out at a beach concert. I was there supporting a girlfriend who was a backup dancer for one of the performers. It was scalding outside that day. I became dehydrated, which caused me to faint. Josh was not even hanging out with me, but I noticed him watching me earlier that day. When I came to, I realized that it was him who stepped up to help me. I thought he looked like a Spanish version of a young Elvis Presley, and I fell for him.

The first time I had dinner with my new family, we had steak, rice, and beans: a traditional Latin meal, *bestake con arroz y frijoles*. Naturally, as we all sat down to eat, I picked up the silverware on the table. As I was chomping away, doing my thing over my plate, I slowly looked up to find that everyone was staring at me. It was as if I was eating with real aliens, not just illegal ones! It felt like someone pressed the slow motion button as I politely put down my fork and knife. I realized then that the utensils were not for the steak, but just for the rice and beans. The knife was decorative, I suppose. I mean, what was I thinking? Why use a fork and knife when I could eat like an animal? When I think back, I must have really believed that I loved him, because his situation went far beyond poor eating habits. He lived in a house that was, by my American standards, absolutely horrifying. When the lights were turned on in the kitchen, mice would scatter from every corner. There were cockroaches, and the house sat right in the heart of Overtown, one of Miami's hardest ghettos.

Eventually, I called that place home with Josh and his family, leaving Nickie and what was left of my normality behind. It was not long after moving in with Josh that my father came to visit me. He came pulling up in his fancy Jaguar and spent about an hour with me. He sat there, looking around at the closet sized room that I was sleeping in, and he tried to convince me to return home with him. The thing is who tries to rationalize with a 17-year-old who, at that point, was lost in a deep dark pit? He should have forced me, but in his heart, he was doing what he thought was best. He was trying to talk to me like an adult, and tough love had become a large part of his parenting after I left him. He started to receive counseling through groups like Al-Anon, Over Compulsive Disorder Anonymous, and a one on one therapist. Those programs encourage people to connect with those they have hurt, or been hurt by, so that had not been the first time he reached out. He went out of his way one other time.

Before I left my mother, my father came to visit me in Sunrise, Florida. It was close to my sixteenth birthday, and we went for a long walk together in a park. He cried, and asked for my forgiveness. However, I was already so angry at him, and I could not bring myself to forgive him. I did not even know how to. His words were empty to me. He spent the following year trying to convince me to go to Ala-Teen meetings, a support group for kids that have an alcoholic parent. I went to a few of them, but only because it was a quick twenty bucks. (He paid me every time I went.) Throughout that year, we would have lunch together, but our conversations were tainted by things like "I love you, *but* . . . I want to do this for you, *but*. . . That is great that you did this, *but* . . ." I could only hear him through a negative mindset, so all I heard was the conjunction "but." I sadly could not hear his words within the realm of a father wanting his daughter to see the wrong choices she was making. My hearing was clouded by a twisted anger, and the road that I was traveling on gave me a false sense of fulfillment.

Generally, most children don't just run away unless they are pushed away. That is why I believe my father was somewhat remorseful the day he came to visit me in Miami, just like that day at the park. Deep down inside, he knew his behavior toward me as a child contributed to my current circumstances. He went out of his way twice, and both attempts allowed him to feel justified. Tough love was all about making sure there was no enabling going on. His small gestures, such as paying my rent and bribing me to do what he wanted, were techniques that did not show me he actually cared. I needed a hero, a father, a man who, during my darkest moments, would love me unconditionally, with compassion. His next actions showed his love was truly conditional. He made it very clear that day in Miami that I was not only out of his last will and testament, but that he no longer had a daughter. He was not going to leave money to a drug user and her illegal boyfriend, and I suppose, he lost all hope for me and my life.

The thing was, living in Overtown with Josh was not a safe place, as I was fully aware. Four guys attacked me one night.

This neighborhood was so rough that a cop slowly drove by and saw me getting attacked, but kept going. I could not rat on the guys either because it would have meant issues for Josh's family. That is the reason they sent me away for a bit of time. I was lost and scared when they sent me away. I did not know where to turn, and it took everything inside of me, but I went to my father's house that night. For the first time since the age of 12, I felt broken. In that one moment, my dad had every opportunity to redeem himself and rescue his little girl. After all, this was only a couple months after he visited me. It was late on a weekend, and when he answered the door, he failed to notice that I had bruises all over from being attacked. I was crying and begging for him to forgive me this time, and for him to take me in. However, he was too busy having dinner with my brother and his girlfriend from college. I had disturbed their nice normal evening, and as he shut the door in my face, I realized he truly meant what he said the day he left me in Miami. He didn't have a daughter anymore. There was no compassion, no love, no concern. It was, "You made your bed, now lie in it!" Slam! I was seventeen years old! To me, all his asking for forgiveness was proven empty that night. His actions showed that he wanted nothing to do with me, and he meant it. I fell to the ground, just wanting to die. I contemplated taking my life all night . . . In my young mind, my father never loved me, and my mother was a hypocritical drug addict. I slept in my car and struggled with where to turn for days. Eventually, Josh's family decided that they would move, and I returned to them.

MARRIAGE...REALLY?!

My journey with Josh was one of the hardest I have had to overcome in my life. He had already fathered a child with another young girl, and he wasn't taking care of either of them. He denied that poor baby was even his, and why he chose to take me in, I had no clue. He may have been a teenager too, but he did not go to school and was living it up. He worked during the day in construction, and on the side he stole cars and gutted them. He owned a machine that would scratch off the VIN number, and I can still see him driving the cars away with only a cement block to sit on.

His sister was dating a Cuban gangster. This was about 1991, and the residue of the 80s was still lingering in the drug world of South Florida. This guy, who ended up in prison, spent his time robbing other well-established thugs. I remember them plotting in secret about how they would map out their attack. I was never part of the conversations, but my nosy self would try to listen from another room. He attempted to get even Josh involved, but he refused, oddly enough. This guy would come home with bags of drugs and counterfeit money like you see on NCIS. We, the whole family, would rummage through the bags as if it was Christmas morning, and Santa Claus had forgotten his goodies in our house. Josh's mother and I would party hard with each other, taking lines of cocaine like candy. His younger brother (who was neglected worse than I was growing up) and I became comforts to each other for a short time. Outside of Josh, he was the only other one that spoke English well. His sister and I became close over time, and with my broken Spanish, we did many things together. She was the local money lender, and we would go around collecting it with interest from all those who borrowed. God only knows what happened to those who didn't pay. Her boyfriend at one point felt threatened by me, and like a fly that has no clue it's about to be smacked into the window of a moving car, I suddenly had a gun pointed at my head. He was ready to pull the trigger. I stood there so still. I don't think anything ever again had me stand so still. I did not say a word. Tears began to flow slowly from my eyes. I thought it was over for me. I did not understand a thing that was going on, but he lowered the gun, and I dropped to the floor. It was not long after that day that I started spending random evenings out. During that time, I ran into my first crush from years earlier, and we began to hang out from time to time. On one particular instance, I stayed out the whole night. When I got home the next day, I learned that the Cuban drug dealer that held a gun to my head was behind bars. Cops came, raided the house, and took him away. Once again, God protected me from experiencing even deeper trouble, such as being murdered.

Outside of my rape, Josh was the first guy that I was intimate with. The hard knock life I was living allows for what comes next to be a given. It did not take long before I was pregnant. The first pregnancy with Josh was when I was sixteen, and still at my mom's house. My mother begged me to abort the baby. All the reasons she gave me made complete sense at the time. Plus, I was scared and although I never listened to my mother, this time, I did. She was there in a moment of need, but she may not have necessarily been the right person to listen to. Nevertheless, I killed my baby, who would have been 24 years old today. Anyone who has ever had a pregnancy knows that there is absolutely life within them from the moment they conceive. I could feel the life within me. My body was not the same, no longer belonging to just myself. I have come to learn that there is no such thing as "just a fetus," and a baby who has yet to be born is just as helpless as a baby who has been, if not more so. In the end, it is always a person's choice; no law will ever prevent that, just like it is our choice to believe in God even if it is the work of the Spirit. We learn from history that when we had a law preventing abortions, women still went around it, and many lost their lives. For myself, no one *forced* me, even if my mother *convinced* me. I went forth, and I take full responsibility for my choice of killing my child. I say with deep remorse that this would not be the last time I carried his child. When I was seventeen and living with him, I became pregnant again; however, Josh had a bad habit of hitting me. He struck me over things as small as my inability to drive a stick shift, and it was over that exact issue that he began shoving me. The fight got ugly. In his culture, it was a natural thing to do as a man, so I miscarried our second child due to his barbaric ways. The following year, once I was eighteen, and we were married, I got pregnant again. This time, I felt in my heart that I would have the opportunity to hold my baby. Josh liked to go out, though, disappearing most weekends. I made the mistake of thinking it was the right thing to do by going to look for him. I found him - in a crack house back in Overtown - in the heart of the ghetto we once lived in. He dragged me out into the street and beat me severely, and left me there. I remember people talking over my body as I felt as if I was going to die. It breaks my heart to say; it was not me who died that night. It was my child. The very next day I was in the hospital having another D&C.

Eventually, his abuse had pushed me far enough. The combination of his brother-in-law threatening to shoot me and the loss of my babies led me to pack my bags and to move to Ft. Lauderdale, intending never to return. However, he followed, along with his beatings. Of course, he promised things would change, and they did not. As the story goes, what did change is I began eating my emotions. Every Friday night, I could sense when he wasn't coming home. I would order in Domino's Pizza and eat the whole pie to fill my emptiness. When he did come home after work, if I did not have his dinner ready for him—even if I were sick—he would shove me around. I could no longer function; although I tried with all that I had. It just was not working. We lasted less than a year as a married couple and less than a few months in Ft. Lauderdale.

I was 19 years old at this point, and I finally decided to go and get my GED. I promised God that I would leave Josh and make a better life for myself if I passed. The results were in; I had passed the test by three points for each subject. I called Antoinette and my father with the good news. To my surprise, not only did she show up for the celebration, but so did my dad. As for the "better life," it would take more than another eight years.

In sum, I see that my family made small efforts to get me the help I needed in order to correct the dysfunctional behavior I began wildly developing. I should've been the child, and they should've been the adults who had all authority over me, *even if I fought them.* Instead, I was left to my own way early on in life, even though I did not know how to make the right choices. With a longing to be loved and wanted, this was only to my demise. Therefore, by the time I was only nineteen years of age, I had been raped, known deceit deeply, and been physically and emotionally abused; in turn, I abused others. I had lost three children, been a heavy drug user, experienced the inside of a gang, married and divorced, had my life threatened, experienced a real drug lord, spent and used his spoils, contemplated my death . . . The list goes on.

Along the way, I met many kids who had suffered at the hands of their parents on all different levels of abuse. Together we set out to care for one another. Many of those kids in their own right were outcasts and went through very dark times. Although they had elements of having to grow up fast, they—to some extent at least—remained kids. It was the neglected, like me, that endured the streets. Sadly, this is a circumstance that happens too often in the United States, and too many end up homeless, actually living on the streets. If it were not for my own desire for comfort, I would have ended up on the streets too. Each step I took, I wholeheartedly believed that I was making the best choice according to what I perceived my options to be. I went out from my father's home and into the world, doing the best I could with the marbles that I had been given. Through those experiences, I made tight friendships, rolled with the high rollers, and shacked with the scum of the earth. I put my life on the line every day without realizing the dangerous line I was walking.

Herein lies the incredible poetry of the whole timeline from ages 13 to 19. My mother, in the midst of her stupor, made a few good choices. One of them happens to be the day she gave me a Bible. It was a pink children's picture Bible, and she even had my name engraved on the front cover. I carried it with me throughout my whole experience. In it, the year before I left my father, I wrote a prayer and put it within the pages. I wrote in my grammatically deficient way for God to give me strength. I still have it, and it reads, "God, please give me stretch." I still take it out from time to time to reflect on it while smiling at my spelling. The point is, it was not luck but the power of a just and holy God that kept me alive through all that I experienced, because I should have died.

8

THE NEW CRAZY

....

As I sat across the table from Antoinette and one of her closest friends, there was a relational disconnect within me. I was no longer that same little girl who set out at fourteen from her father's house. There was a real shift from a mindset of finding happiness to one of emptiness. My experiences had hardened me, but in that special moment with my friend . . . I was just content to see her face. The simplicity of just sitting there, surrounded by a place I once knew, brought a sigh of release. It was there, sitting in a popular eatery, chowing down on chicken wings and sipping on soda, that I shared a condensed version of what my marriage to Josh was like. We were there less than an hour, and Antoinette and her friend began to encourage me to leave the abusive situation. I may have had no idea how to relate to the world, but I knew that I could not stay in the one I was in. I was already ready to make the transition, so their motivation encouraged me to take that last step I was so terrified to take.

As I returned to the culture I once knew, and left the abusive world of my ex-husband, I had a renewed sense of freedom. The air that surrounded me felt fresh for the first time in years, and I even felt a change in my breathing. I was able to take a deep breath knowing that I was not going to feel the wrath of Josh any longer. I felt free, like a bird being let out of a cage knowing that I no longer had an abusive husband. It was as if I was recovering from an awful illness. The thing is, I had removed myself from the sickness, but ultimately I was still left with the internal issues that drove me toward the abuse in the first place.

Sadly, at nineteen, I lacked both the ability to identify the real cause of my circumstances and the knowhow to engage the world sober. Having never been taught how to deal with my emotions that seemed to rule my thoughts, I was stuck mentally. When I looked deep into my soul, all I saw was an emptiness, which was as dark as night. I found that I only knew how to fill all my doubts, insecurities, and pain through things that were mind altering. Drugs allowed me to push everything deep down. They took my cares away. I woke up for the next few years with a joint and a line of cocaine: a nice and hearty breakfast for champions, I always said.

There were several familiar faces in my transition, but soon I found myself surrounded by a new type of people. I basically went from gangs and thieves among the Latin community to a passion for rock-n-roll and Harleys. I took a step horizontally, thinking it was vertical, and the dreams of a fairytale future were lost by the time I was nineteen years old. Without me even realizing it, my coldness, or more likely numbness toward the world, drove my movements. I think the only thing that brought me through this next period of life was the desire for something better that had been pushed deep down into my heart. At the moment, though, walking out of what I did, I did not know how to be anything but what I had become . . . damaged!

AN ATTEMPT

It was 1993 when I left Josh, and the grunge scene was at its height of popularity, having reached the East Coast from Seattle. I had made my horizontal move from the Latin Express, tucking that time away as if it never happened. The music of the time spoke to my soul, and it fell right into place with my affinity towards rock music, drugs, and just not caring one bit. I picked up the nickname Hippie Girl. The term, however, was most definitely redefined for a new era. Instead of Janis Joplin, it was Joan Jett. Instead of flowers in my hair, I had a cigarette lighter with a metal chain hanging from my side. Instead of Birkenstocks, I wore combat boots most days. I did wear Patchouli oil, but I wore it to hide the smell of pot. I even disgraced my Jewish heritage by obtaining several tattoos and piercings. I suppose my mother's father, who had Cherokee Indian heritage, would have been proud, though. (He is my one non-Jewish grandparent, and I seemed to have inherited his distinctions. I get asked all the time if I'm Native American.) As the story continues, I hit the grunge scene hard, ready to throw my life to the wind.

It was during those days that I often heard the expression, "Youth is wasted on the young." I never understood it until I looked backward on my life as a grown woman. When I reflect upon those days, I may be able to acknowledge that poor parental skills led me down a dark path. The thing is, with mature eyes, I also recognize that there were subtle but real opportunities to change that presented themselves to me along the way that I passed up. An example of an opportunity was when my father offered to pay my college tuition. He had no strings attached to the offer either, and I was allowed the freedom to run my life without his two cents. That may have been the downfall though because I needed encouragement and strict discipline in my life. I may have been nineteen with 5 to 6 years of raising myself under my belt, but that was just it . . . I lacked mature judgment. My father felt he was doing good by me, but how can a blind person map out his or her own route without first being given guidance concerning the right path to choose?

Figuring life out on my own has ultimately been a blessing in disguise because I do not allow fear of change to hinder me any longer. At that time, however, my worldview was tainted, and as I graced the front door of the community college, I felt like John Bender from the Breakfast Club; a complete outsider with all my insecurities rushing towards me. My placement test prevented me from starting credited classes, and all at once, I was back to being that "slow learning" little girl who had no idea where to begin as she stared down at her schoolwork.

The age-old saying goes "Can't see the forest for the trees." That was what life was like for me. I had this incredible opportunity that many never get, but I was too trapped within my fears to ask for help. I did not even know how to ask for help, and I was blind to the help that was in front of me. I did not comprehend that, if I really wanted to achieve something, I had to work hard through my educational limitations. I cut off my nose to spite my face without even realizing that was what I was doing. Drugs, Rock and Roll, and kicking back had a much better appeal to me. Therefore, from ages nineteen to twenty-three, I forfeited the chance I had to get a free education. Regrettably, this was one of those real opportunities wasted in my youth.

BORDERLINE

Soon after my divorce, I developed some truly strange relationships, and one of them drew me into a very dark experience. It almost left me mentally ruined for life. When I first attempted to attend Broward Community College (BCC), I bumped into my childhood neighbor, Sheila. I was surprised to see her at BCC. She was the all-American girl, and I figured she would have been in the movies by then or off at some expensive college. She was the cheerleader next door who modeled and got small parts in films. Ironically, or I should say sadly, life had thrown her a curve ball when she was not looking. She got hit hard! The divorce of her parents broke her heart, and her father practically left her at the curb. She took it deeply, rightfully so, and she and I connected right away on common grounds. All it took was hearing her story for me to feel a connection. I immediately brought her into my world.

When I was around my inner circle of friends, I let my guard down. When my walls were down, due to being very high, I did not tend to pick up on things quickly, and my lack of education left a deficiency in my speech. My girls respected me too much to make fun of me as I often mispronounced or misread words. Sheila, on the other hand, sometimes enjoyed feeding off that. From my perspective, growing up next door to me, she also knew all my weak spots. It was not long until her grade school attitude toward me surfaced from time to time. I was a perfect target for someone who reveled in picking on a person's inabilities, as she did. She loved me, but she enjoyed playing mind games with me too. I did not like it as a child, nor did I like it then. It would cause me to feel an illness in my stomach, and it was with Sheila that my mental condition changed for the worse.

One particular evening Sheila, another close friend Lorelai, and I dropped some acid and did a few lines of cocaine in my apartment. I do not remember our plans for that evening; all I remember is that they thought it would be fun to mess with me while I was still getting ready. They enjoyed teasing me because they knew it always got to me, and on this night took what they thought was innocent much too far. Let me just say, it did not go very well, as they played on my rejection issues by pretending to have left me while heavily drugged out. To their credit, they did not know my internal struggles firsthand, but they knew it would rouse me if they pretended to have left me. Why else mess with someone, other than to get a reaction? I knew the answer well from how I treated people to a different degree. Their actions may not have been such a big deal to a sober mind, but after two hits of acid and some lines of cocaine, it is a big deal to provoke a person in any fashion. Accordingly, when they jumped out of the closet, they scared me to such a degree that I could not cope with my thoughts. I kicked them out and ended up sitting in my apartment paranoid for over a week. I felt so lost thinking that someone was going to come and kill me. I sat looking out my window like a mad woman for days. I was so angry for the longest time at both of them. It was because of that night, and several other frightening episodes on acid, all coincidentally with Sheila, I border-lined insane.

The heavy use of the acid, with the wrong people, transformed my drug use from all fun and feeling good to paranoid and destructive. I began to read into *everything*, which didn't help my relationship with anyone within that specific season. At one point, I could not even drive down a street without thinking there was some conspiracy going on. Even Antoinette and Nickie sensed a difference in me as if I was mentally off somewhere in my thoughts. I ended up struggling for a couple of years to a significant degree with being around people. It was only when I felt comfortable, like my times with Antoinette that I could cut loose. Even then, I had an odd perspective of what was going on around me. I did not trust a single person, and I would always return to a place in my mind of thinking that they wanted to hurt me in some form or fashion. I honestly believe that because I have always had a strong willed mind, I was able to rationalize myself out of that psychosis after some time. It took being sober for that to happen entirely though.

In the end, my last time using acid was after a road trip with Sheila from Florida to Virginia. It was like being in a horror movie, as I stood in a public bathroom seeing my face like a skeleton in the mirror. Once again my strong willed mind, thank God, was able to keep me from accepting that as reality, and at twenty years of age, I had escaped almost becoming locked up in a funny farm. I never touched that form of acid again.

OH THE PLACES YOU'LL GO

The second half of this crazy stage of my life began when I was twenty and living in Oakland Park, a suburb of Ft. Lauderdale. It was there that I met my first serious boyfriend after my divorce. It was a whirlwind relationship that lasted on and off for almost three years, filled with baggage that could take up several chapters. I will never forget the day that guy walked in my front door. It was a typical day in South Florida, the kind where you wanted to hide inside away from the sun because it was smoldering hot. He came over with a mutual friend.

I cannot say that it was a physical attraction for me, even though he was a good-looking young guy. It was much more like two hurting and lost souls colliding as their paths crossed. I can remember when the connection happened as if it was yesterday.

He was leaving, and already standing in the parking lot. I was standing outside of my apartment looking over the railing from the second floor. At that moment, everything around him faded. All I saw were his baby blue eyes as he batted his lashes enough times for me to notice. There was something that spoke to my soul and intrigued me to want to know him, and as he started to come over often, I enjoyed his company. He was passionate, full of ideas, and in my current grunge scene frame of mind, he was a cool looking punk rocker. He looked like a Mad Max character with his shaved head and a long black ponytail, oddly left behind as if someone forgot to shave it off. He had tattoos, and one of them was an anarchy symbol on his arm. He would always say, "Twelve judges and one and half chance in *hades* for justice." He, to put it mildly, strangely intrigued me.

There is one thing I learned from the world that I came out of; many who were there were real outcasts, thrown away by their families. For this reason, it should be no surprise when I share that Eric's story was one that could sadden anyone with a heart towards others. There does come a point in our lives though where we need to take responsibility for how we are choosing to live our lives, no matter what has happened to us. We were just pups back then, however, with chips on our shoulders, drawn to each other in a rebellious movie-like manner. I don't mean a romantic one like *Pride and Prejudice*, either.

He came from a small town in Kansas, and his father was a cop. Whenever he would share about his youth spent running from the police, I could not help but picture him as one of the Dukes of Hazzard boys. He had explained how he had served some hard time behind bars before coming to South Florida, and back then, that knowledge didn't faze me much.

When I met Eric, I was not looking for him. As a matter of fact, I was already interested in a good man, one who was genuinely trying to help me through my struggles. Eric was also fresh out of a relationship, and he had already fathered a baby girl. It was too much for me to handle, but I continued to hang with him despite my intuition. Eric, though, would not take no for an answer, and he was giving me the attention that I wanted. That attention was what got me to budge, so it took only a month before I was caught up in his web. He owned just a couple boxes of stuff and was barely getting by. He had a terrible addiction too, and he found a vulnerable girl who would take him in. A girl, unbeknownst to him, that was still struggling with a mental condition due to those bad acid trips.

Eric was never an epic love for me. He was a profoundly strange reality where I got lost emotionally and mentally, and we partied to the core together. We were, in many ways, a very mild version of Micky and Mallory, from the movie *Natural Born Killers*. Those who knew us well called us by those names because we looked like them and we were pretty hardcore together. We would walk through intense mosh pits filled with hundreds of people, and they would part like we were Moses crossing the Red Sea. I have no clue why, other than the fact that cocaine made us feel like we were larger than life. We put out an energy that demanded something in return.

Our first year together was our golden year. We had a blast, and our souls had a unique connection between my insanity and his outlook on life. We were in it, not to win it, but we were content without a care in the world. However, all that changed after we had been dating for a year and I began to draw close to a lady I met at one of my dive spots. She looked like a female version of Sam Kinison, with frizzy blonde hair and a terrible electric shock. She thought of herself as a witch but called herself a rhyming expletive. That comment always made me laugh. She wore crystals, played with tarot cards, and performed magical incantations. I was so hungry to discover the truth on my journey towards God that I became mesmerized by her antics. I would hold onto everything she said to me as if she was speaking an absolute truth.

With drugs in my system, a mental condition, and her convincing me of some strange ideologies, someone needed to lock me up and throw away the key. During my visits, she would begin doing whatever spell she was conjuring, and the door would swing open by itself. There is no doubt that we conjured up 'something' together. My very dark path compelled me towards her, and it was not long before she had me convinced that I needed to leave Eric. She did not just put a *hex* on me; she put a *hexadecimal*! (Only computer nerds got that one!) Needless to say, my relationship with her ruined my relationship with Eric.

A Time Apart

The timetable of events are a bit fuzzy when it comes to Eric and me beyond our first year, but after I had left him the first time, it was not going to be my last partnership with him. When we parted ways after a year, though, I began to hang out with Daria, the Kinison look-alike, a lot more than any of my other friends. She fulfilled my desire for darkness, when compared to Lorelai, Nickie, and even Sheila. Antoinette was the one I brought around Daria the most, and I'm willing to bet that she and I experienced some of our funniest shared memories during this awkward phase of my life with this strange lady.

Also during this time, I got my tattoos and became very close with a biker who had close ties with some of the local *Hells Angels*. They scared me, but I still hung out with some of them occasionally, that is if my friend was around. I remember giving one of them a ride home one night. As I drove up to the house, there was a large fence around the property that seemed to say "don't think you're seeing what's inside." They called it their "fort."

Outside of our witchery connection and our strange talks about life, the darkest moment I had during my relationship with Daria was when I met this scrawny, "grunged-out" kid. He happened to be close to a group of people I knew from my youth, and she encouraged me to be with him. He already had a girlfriend, but that did not stop either of us from pursuing a relationship. I treated him like a rag doll, but only because I did not care. I was dating several people at that time, but I eventually did give him more attention. Without going down that rabbit trail, the numbness of my life is best summed up in what I am about to share. I ended up getting pregnant from this guy, and neither of us cared enough to talk even about it. As a mindless gesture—like a zombie—I went to have an abortion. In my mind, it was as simple as going to the dentist for a teeth cleaning. I drove myself there. As the women in the clinic asked me questions, their voices sounded like Charlie Brown's teacher, and I just wanted to get through to the other side. That night I was drinking and drugging as if nothing had happened. If that doesn't define how far lost I was, I don't know what else would.

RECONNECTED

After the abortion, I started to miss my ex-boyfriend, Eric, and I begged him to take me back. He, by this time, had found a whole new group of friends and plenty of new girlfriends. He took me back, but only as a toy, for he found solace in the arms of other girls. There was no doubt about that, as his actions were in plain sight. I never believed him when he told me that "I was seeing things." But for a while, I stayed with him despite his treatment. It was very clear from the outset that we were never going to get back to being what we were before. It was different now, and in time, I became enraged with jealousy.

Probably the pivotal moment that best demonstrated the dysfunction of our relationship was the night we went to my favorite spot to get some drinks. As soon as we got there, he made a beeline for his new crowd of friends. Other girls were flirting with him, and he was not stopping them. In retaliation, I thought I would be a wise guy, so I flirted with another guy. In hindsight, that did not go over very well with Eric. He was very protective of me, no matter how little he seemed to care for me, so he started a fight with the guy. When all was said and done, Eric had been stabbed so severely that he almost lost his life. He emerged with a permanent scar, and his opponent ended up doing some hard time in jail for it.

I remember sitting in the hospital surrounded by all his new friends, feeling like a foreigner. I was in shock, and this event did not bring Eric and me back together in the way one would think near-death experiences do. Our "relationship" came to a head when I went to check on him after he got out of the hospital. He was so angry with me when I got there that we ended up getting into a huge domestic fight, which landed us both in jail. It was at that moment, riding in the back seat of that police car beside me, that he began to cry. It was like a light went off in his head. Looking at me, he realized what we were doing to each other. He then begged the police officer to let me go, pleading that I was innocent. I'll never forget the tears in his eyes as he asked me for forgiveness.

I remained behind bars for a solid seven days. My parents refused to get me out, and I did not have the money to bail myself out. I was even transported to another facility, experiencing the sheer humiliation of the process one goes through getting booked, shackled, and suited. To this day, I don't know how this happened, but when I went to my arraignment, the judge yelled, "What is this? Who are you? Get out of my courtroom and don't come back!" I did not even have a moment to answer any of his questions! It could've only been one of two things: either the grace of God moved my father to get me off the hook, or the cop believed what Eric had said about my innocence. I was led out of the courtroom so thankful that I was never convicted of domestic abuse.

During this whole fiasco, I was already pregnant by Eric. After the jail incident, both he and my mother talked me into getting an abortion. I was so scared and angry . . . and with much resistance and regret in my heart, I killed yet another innocent child out of pure selfishness. Not being in as dark of a place as I was the last time, I was somewhat conscious of my actions. I was upset enough afterward to not be able to even look at Eric anymore. He, on the other hand, expressed a desire to get back to our foundation; but after everything we had been through, I just could not give it any more effort. Meanwhile, Daria had moved to North Carolina, and I found myself packing my bags to follow her there.

Right before I left for North Carolina, however, Eric and I ran into a young girl who came from a Christian family. She and I met during a critical time for me; I had experienced a spiritual nightmare with Daria, had lost my roots in the Jewish faith, and I was spiritually dehydrated. I was desperate for something to believe in. I was already a "tree hugger," and I readily accepted whatever sounded good. She brought Eric and me to her family's house, and they led us in reciting a "sinner's prayer." However, if you would have asked me to explain the gospel, I would have only grunted back the exact words I heard. Anyone with a discerning heart would have been able to tell that I was not aware of what I was saying. When I sat in Church that following Sunday listening to the pastor, he made me so angry. He was harping on about abortions, and I had just had one. The things he said made my insides burn as if I was within the walls of a judgment camp. The firing squad was aiming right at me, and after a couple of Sundays with them, I turned my back.

Last chance

My mother and I spent time together often, after my jail experience. We didn't have a great relationship, but we got along well enough. She even drove with me up to North Carolina when I moved there. We had a blast! We certainly knew how just to be friends, when we were not trying to be mother and daughter.

When I moved to North Carolina for a very brief season, I walked into a proverbial snake trap and got bitten. My experience with Daria was a story right out of Jerry Springer, so I left her within a couple of months of moving there. I remained in North Carolina, though, and I found a new community of misfits. Having come from South Florida, and experiencing all that I had, I had a much too high opinion of myself. It was there that I was taken down a few notches. I found all the same trouble to get myself into, and I partied just as hard. It was there that I first smoked Crank, and started using crystal meth. Deep down, though, I began to want freedom from the choices I was making. In many ways, I believe my Christian experience planted a seed. Ultimately, at this stage of my life, I was almost twenty-three, and I legitimately began to feel the effects of my life choices sneaking up on me.

Since I was now doing heavier drugs, it should come as no surprise that I had some awful, spiritually dark experiences in

NC. These drove me to pack my bags and visit Florida. Like a pig returns to mud, I went straight to Eric. Although he did not get the excitement in my expression that he was expecting, deep down he was all I wanted, even after all we had been through. I begged him to come back to NC with me. And despite the fact that he was dating another girl, he left her behind and joined me. Before long, he began cheating once again. This time, it was too close for comfort. I felt like this was his revenge for me leaving him the first time. Whatever his reason, he found himself in the arms of my boss at the club I worked at, and both of them lied to my face. The mental games had me lost for words. In my naivety, I thought if I took him away from the girl he was seeing, things would be different. However, when we got back to Florida, he made it clear that we could never return to the glory of our relationship. I finally came to the realization that *nothing* was ever going to change with him as long as I stayed in the relationship. I packed my bags once again, and I disappeared, this time changing my phone number. I finalized our relationship.

THE TRANSITION

I was twenty-three when I finally left Eric for good. Once again, during a major transition in my life, I turned to my father. He had recently called me to say that he had accepted Jesus as his Lord and Savior. My dad asked me, "Did you know that he wasn't born in December?" Today I chuckle about that, but back then it made no sense. Santa Claus is who Christians celebrated in December, so what did Jesus have to do with it? My father and I slowly built a renewed relationship after that phone call. I believe that call opened the door for me to lean on him once I was truly free of Eric.

I was ready to find a better place for myself in life. I was tired. I did not have anything left in me that wanted to fight. I was ready to get my life straight, even though I had no idea where to start. My father and I began to grow close. There was a glimpse of light on the horizon signaling that we were going to start healing our wounds, and I was ready to make him proud. He enrolled me in college, bought me a new car, and offered to pay my rent in an apartment close to his house. All I had to do was leave my 'career of choice' during that period of time, get a real job, and attend college. I was finally ready! He even convinced me to get into real estate.

While I was waiting for the new college year to start, I spent weeks studying to receive a real estate license. The girl who, barely had a GED, had never read a book and had done enough drugs to permanently damage her mind, finally had a real drive for the first time in her life. I gave it all I had. I read, even without fully understanding. All I knew was that my father was going to take me under his wing, and I could sense that it was real. He was a new man, and I could tell that there was something very calm about him. He wasn't that wise guy I left years earlier.

I was so disappointed the day I took my exam and failed by one lousy, little point. Me, one point away! It was quite an accomplishment, but I could not see past disappointing my father. When I got to his house, he answered the door ready to celebrate with me. He had his arms open wide, and when I showed him my test results, he was so encouraging. He told me, "It is perfectly OK, Kiddo. I failed mine the first few times too. Just keep on trying, you will get there." Tragically, a week later he passed away. The pain and guilt that overcame me was like Mt. Vesuvius overwhelming the town of Pompeii with her lava. Desolation was all that was left. I have never felt as alone in my life as I felt in that very moment. After all those years of discord, my father and I were finally on the right path. My head was even getting clear, as I was no longer using hardcore drugs. I had come to the place where all I wanted was my dad, and for us to move forward.

9

COLD AS ICE

During my rock-n-roll era, as I call it, my family and I were not close in the way a typical family is. Some of us talked, but we didn't necessarily engage one another. In reality, I was not that close to anyone. Drugs drove my emotions and thoughts, and my relationships were filtered through an altered state of mind. I could have tried to be a healthy part of my family at that point, but I did not know how to. I was lacking in so many ways and consequently from nineteen to twenty-three I lived in a whirlwind.

I had not spoken to my brother since he left for college, and we would not connect again until after our father's passing. He was a good kid, and like many young adults that go away to college, he was immersed in his college fraternity world. He was living the average American life, having great experiences, traveling, and making friends that would last a lifetime. The last thing on his mind was picking up the phone and reaching out to his wayward little sister. We had never been that close anyway.

In the scheme of things, we were together but for a moment in our younger years. We have lived entirely separate and certainly distinctive lives since then. We even have contrasting points of views concerning our childhood relationship. Where he feels he was an emotionally healthy constant towards me, I feel that we were typical siblings, minus the emotionally healthy intimacy. Needless to say, from the time I ran away at fourteen through the age of twenty-three when my father passed away, we were strangers in the night— sailing on two very different ships.

I have often wondered if it would have made a difference had he reached out to me. For all I know it may have, depending on how hard he tried. Throughout my childhood, I had always loved and looked up to him from afar, but by the age of twelve, my worldview was strangled because of years of feeling completely unwanted and neglected. This emotional suffocation caused me nothing but hardship, and perhaps culminated in the place I was at psychologically when I got divorced. For this reason, I had no idea how to connect with those I felt had previously rejected me. I only knew how to reach out to strangers, perpetually hoping that the next person I would meet would be the one who would want me forever. Thus, we went nine years without talking to each other, aside from the time I showed up at my father's front door at the age of seventeen.

I spoke with my mother and visited her from time to time. She even went out of her way to visit me a few times, which I appreciated. We seemed to get along well because we didn't have anything meaningful to converse about. I would be stoned, so it was like we were on the same wavelength. Once I moved out of her home, our brief dysfunctional time together from fourteen to sixteen was in the past. Our relationship, although we saw each other and talked, really did not rekindle on a deeper level until I was about twenty-four and in college.

As for my father, he was there for me when I first got a divorce, and even to this day I do not take that lightly. He was present with me at the courthouse and helped me with the paperwork. During my divorce proceedings, we did sense the beginning of a rekindled relationship. I still have, for sentimental reasons, all his notes to me during that process. In the moment, I could not see that his intentions were good though. I could not wrap my mind around the person he had become, and I was wrong in how I dealt with his words and actions then. He may have still been a man with a lot of emotional issues, but he was trying the best he knew how to reach me at that moment. This is why I miss him with my whole heart. I find myself wishing every day that he could have lived long enough to see the person I have become. Once I got sober, I spent many days grieving within my soul, due to the fact that my father passed away only knowing the person I used to be.

A DEEPER LOOK

My brother told me once that I would have made my life simple had I bided my time and not run away. I spent many days, especially throughout my thirties, mulling over those words. Many days would pass where I yearned to be one of those people who just rode the wave of life like he did. I was just not built that way. I felt too deeply. I had too much heart and passion driving my spirit. I was a fighter by nature, so through my restless youth, I fought everything and everyone.

It took me a long time to learn how to control my natural instincts. During my early years, when I was out of control, my instincts always got the best of me. They dominated my mind and played a complex game with my emotions. Those who passed through my life expressed rational reasoning to me, but I tended to believe myself over the words of others.

I dealt with life encompassed with a wall of my making, and

my hearing was stuck in defensive mode. Defending myself was a knee-jerk reaction, like when a doctor tests your reflexes. The reaction was the same whenever I felt threatened. When I was sober, it was hard to talk to me about me. Since I had never worked through the things I had gone through, I understood most words from a victim's perspective.

The fire that raged in my heart turned into a passion that burned deep within my soul, and it assumed the form of anger towards the world around me. This made the fervor within me pick a path that was unknowingly hard. Had I known better, I would have chosen the path of renewal while my dad was alive. However, I thank God every day that my mother has lived long enough to see me today. The truth of the matter is, I did not know how to pick a healthy road even if it was staring right at me. My role models, those I loved most, sent me down the destructive path as a result of their own destructive lives. Due to the lack of nurture I received in my formative years, their attempts to stop me did not register. I was lost in a dangerous world, and my family's lack of emotional health enabled me to remain lost. After all, we only do things to the degree we ourselves know how to.

You see, I have taken responsibility for my choices the day my choices as an adult became my responsibility. Even so, I don't beat myself up over the life I lived during my teenage years that led me to the decisions I made after my divorce. It was during my youth that I most needed a father and mother who would have at least attempted to protect me from some of the experiences I had. I think every parent messes up, but not every parent releases his or her child into such havoc without a fight. I strongly believe that it is a parent's responsibility to protect and nurture their children while teaching them the difference between right and wrong.

The thing is, my father may well have recognized that I was on the wrong track and needed help, but at the end of the day, he did not know how to fix me. In fact, it was impossible for him to repair that which he had broken . . . because he too was broken. It took a lot of effort for me to step outside of my victimized worldview and finally realize that I was indeed a victim of emotional abuse. It was freeing just to accept it instead of *defending* it. When I realized the obstacle in my thinking that kept me from perceiving the world through positive lenses, I was also able to recognize that in my father as well. He was victimized in his life, too. Like so many families, our family had fallen into a vicious cycle of abuse and just like he wore that reality, so did I. As an emotionally stunted young girl, I could not grasp the reality that my life was going nowhere. I just thought the world was one big messed up place, and that I was in it, alone and doing my best.

As a child, I felt rejected, unloved, worthless, ugly, mentally challenged, and without a family. These feelings followed me into my young adult life. Looking back, I see that all I needed was for someone to keep showing up consistently, and through their actions demonstrating that they were with me and for me. I will say this: my father did many things right, he certainly did, and I would be wrong to rob him of his efforts. There was just a missing key to my well-being that was the result of neglect, which ultimately influenced how I felt about myself. I was not born feeling that way; those feelings were developed in me by how I was treated.

My discernment was right. My father had wronged me, but I was becoming no better than him in how I treated others. Holding onto the pain was counterproductive, though, and I continually created dysfunction in my life. I had to let go of the pain, of not feeling wanted or loved. From this new angle, I was able to see that my poor father was a deeply hurting man.

Once I accepted that my pain and hurt was inflicted by a man who was dealing with the bad things that happened to him as a child, I could see that he did not set out to wrong me. He was not neglecting me on purpose; his behavior was an overflow of his own hurt. I am not justifying or excusing his awful parenting skills. After all, he was the adult, and there were plenty of examples for him to have learned from and to know better. My father was an adult immobilized from the pain in his youth, though. My eyes have been opened to that cycle. Having forgiveness for a man who did not know how to engage with life due to his suffering has taught me to recognize when I too am hurting others based on my own sore spots. In that, there is freedom to love my neighbor as myself!

Friends—The Family of the Neglected

I was searching high and low to find a place where I could obtain peace, love, and a family. The closest I could get to that peace was getting high, and the only love I felt was from my relationships. As for family, it was never a reality. It breaks my heart to think about how I used to picture myself alone, even when I was in a serious relationship and surrounded by friends. I always had a vision of myself standing on a dock wearing a flowing dress, holding out a drink to the waves of the ocean as the moon gently glistened upon the water. I would toast the wind, content in my lonely life.

I may not have had blood family swirling around me, but I was never really alone. I always had many friends; however, misery loves company. True friendships were healthy, like the one I had with Antoinette, but overall, I tended to attract others who were just like me. Together, we put our troubled lives to the side, and we partied like rock stars. The underground became my world during those immediate years following my divorce. It would have taken my whole nuclear family to come together in a show of absolute, unconditional love towards me to make a difference by this time. A selfless act of authentically trying on their part could have brought me out of the emotional and mental turmoil that my survival had become based on. In the end, the people in my family knew the path that I went down, but it was easier to judge me than to try and rescue me. I suppose we can term their actions 'tough love,' but I choose to see it as neglect. I don't buy into the philosophy that says you have to let your children make their choices when those choices are ruining their lives. Instead, I believe that you call them frequently, invite them over, and go out of your way to be a part of their lives. However, not everyone lives by these rules, especially in our individualistic, self-serving society. It is too much work. That is today's philosophy.

Ultimately, when I reached out to my friends from my high school years, it was the faithful few that showed up faster than I could hang up the phone. Nickie and Antoinette were among the first I reconnected with, and then my friend, Lorelai. These three women are still very dear to my heart. Today we are more than friends; we are family. By the time of my divorce, each one of them had discovered new roads to explore in life, and I was more than ready to join them. They fulfilled my emotional cravings, and I found myself splitting my time amongst them, each of them providing me with such different experiences.

NICKIE

I did not understand why at the time, but when I reunited with Nickie, all my insecurities came rushing forth. Although these insecurities revolved around my outward appearance, they certainly stemmed from how I felt on the inside. I had a strong sense of being different, and I was not as glamorous or breathtaking as she and her new friends. She had moved forward from our past, and created a whole world for herself, one that I did not fit into. But like the caring sister she always was towards me, she came alongside me to try and build me up. She opened her entire wardrobe up to me, and although I did not wear that world as confidently as she did, I slipped right in.

Our time together was extraordinary. We rode in limos, drove fancy cars, relaxed on yachts, and wined and dined at all the finest places that Ft. Lauderdale and Miami could offer. I loved being with Nickie. We always got along, with the exception of one fight when we were younger. I believe she taught me much of what I know about the importance of self-care. No matter how low my self-esteem has gotten, all I gleaned from her has crept back into my mind repeatedly, to remind me to care for myself. Today, I add what she taught me about being female to what the Word of God states that I am as His creation, and I am able to stand tall in the midst of my faults.

In what felt like otherworldly experiences, together we dreamed of fame and fortune and went to those spiritual places that I now know not to go. When I was around her, it was truly like leaving reality and escaping into an alternate universe of glamour and beauty, experiencing places that should have only been left to the imagination. I saw much more than I ever should have because of my friendship with this talented and incredibly imaginative woman. I got to hang out with legitimate rock stars. She provided me with life experiences that most people only dream of. It was in those excursions that I gained the confidence never to give up on myself, and always to seek deeper within my soul for a better life. Seeds were planted during those moments, and I believe in my heart of hearts that those journeys of soul searching with Nickie are what ultimately moved me to begin seeking God.

ANTOINETTE

When I hung out with Antoinette, I hung out with a very different crowd. We had your typical young adult fun. This was the closest I got to experiencing what my brother's normal life was like. Antoinette was, and still is, a pillar in my life. She is a rare gem. From the moment she declared she was my friend, she meant it. She comes from a solid family, and her parents raised her exceptionally well. Growing up, in all moments big and small, she was right there. When I got sold out—"sold out sisters" we called ourselves—when I got married, when I lost my babies, when my father died, when I had nowhere to turn, and the list goes on. She was the only friend who was always right there, physically, and ready to come alongside me with unconditional love. It never mattered what was going on in her life; she has always been sacrificial in her friendship. All those who know her confess the same. She is the real thing! She never derailed too far off the straight path, and yet has always had a way of being unreserved. I love her so deeply, and I believe that God allowed her to be in my life to plant a seed of normality.

Now, I must say, we had our fun too. To say the least, we had some crazy adventures together, and if we were to write a book about them, it would be called *The Wacky Adventures of the Traveling Pants*. She was not an angel. Had she been one, she would have never hung out with some of us! However, she was much more grounded than the rest. Reflecting back, I remember there were times her mother wanted to kill us, especially me. I brought some 'colorful influences' into her daughter's life. For instance, there was the time that one of my crazy biker friends, who was very much a big brother to me, invited Antoinette to attend Bike Week in another state. She went. Her mother was lost for words, or should I say her mother had a lot of words! Picture Judge Judy going off in the courtroom – that describes her mother to a T. She was calling around as if her daughter had been kidnapped. (If I were a mom, I would have been doing the same.) This man was not some preppy guy simply having a mid-life crisis. He was a real biker, a man devoted to the road and his tattoo work. To give an example of his demeanor, I will share about the first time we went to eat sushi together.

We rode down to South Beach in Miami one night to a restaurant that was fancy, crowded, and popular. He did not want sushi but, like everyone who knows me, he knew that I loved it. The night was going well as we sat in the packed restaurant, with tables lined up back to back. Our meals had finally arrived at the table, and he spent a good minute looking for a set of proper utensils. I don't know what he was thinking. Perhaps because it was so crowed, he felt it was too much to ask for a set. Instead, he glared down with confusion at the pair of slick, wooden chopsticks nicely placed on his napkin. Then, he did the most embarrassing thing. He shrugged his shoulders, pulled out his knife, and began to enjoy his meal.

Needless to say, he was a bit rough around the edges, and he had Antoinette taking baths in lakes as they roughed it for Bike Week. When she returned, she had an addition to her body in the form of a huge tattoo. I laugh just thinking about the whole story, but at the time, her mother was ready to roll heads. Today, we all joke about it.

Through all our adventures, I do not have one bad memory being with 'my Bologna', as I call her. We had strange and fun times together. She is my girl. She is what family is meant to be like. I love her as a sister and cherish her being in my life during its darkest hours.

LORELAI

My time with Lorelai was unlike my time with anyone else, because we had a unique relationship. The chemistry between us was constantly at odds, yet we continued to be very much a part of each other's lives. We became sisters to each other, bound together under horrible circumstances. If any song described us, it was Wish You Were Here by Pink Floyd. We were "just two lost souls swimming in a fish bowl, year after year, running over the same old ground." What we did find were "the same old fears." The lyrics of that song spoke deeply to my soul back then, and because of our experiences, my love for Lorelai runs deeper than any traditional relationship. The old time saying goes, "you can't pick your family, but you can pick your friends." I believe sometimes we can't even pick our friends, they just show up, and some people are just worth fighting for. I can testify that when clashing personalities have a breakthrough, the relationship turns deep and indestructible. Lorelai is that person to me. Even when we've pulled away from each other; she has always had my heart.

Lorelai came from a broken home as well. Her mother was Austrian, and her father was a Jewish man from Brooklyn. Although her mother raised her, she spent some time with her father while he lived in Mexico. She mesmerized me because she already spoke two languages, and after returning from Mexico, she was fluent in Pan-American Spanish. She had one of those brilliant minds that many people couldn't comprehend. She truly caught onto to things easily. It was one of the reasons, as a lost young girl, I looked up to her.

I will never forget the day she called me with the news her mother had shared with her. The father she thought was her biological dad, the one in Mexico, wasn't. The song Alive by Pearl Jam became the theme of her life, and we would sing it together while thinking about her parental situation. Lorelei was truly left to figure life out on her own. Her story goes deep and is a book in itself. Like me, she suffered from rejection and the pain of abandonment, but with a much deeper spin. We were two hurting little girls trying to make ourselves believe we were fine, and it was actually the rest of the world that needed to change. We found it difficult to get along, as we were both using our survival skills on each other. Our hardness made us clash together like two stones. However, we got something out of being together, so our relationship has lasted on and off throughout our lives.

There was one thing we always agreed on, and that was our journeys to "candy land." Mind you; we were not playing board games. That was just our expression for the drugs we did together. Lorelei was a tremendous dancer, and I was a rocker at heart. We found a happy medium in the "grunge world," a world filled with drugs, music, and dancing.

During the ages of 19 to about 21, my time with Lorelai cannot realistically be compared to the game Candy Land; it was more like Operation, the game that came out in the late 1960s. We took ridiculous risks when we were together, and I don't recall us ever staying sober in each other's presence. The closest was when we were sleeping. We hung out with everyone and anyone. I got into the business of selling paper acid, and we were mixing it with cocaine. It is quite clear that we were not at home mentally. Our physical bodies were there, but our minds were definitely elsewhere.

There was no depth to our reason for living; we just wanted the next high and good rock-n-roll. We had off the wall mottos, and it was during this period that Lorelei introduced me to a new world that further deteriorated my mental state. While I was married to Josh, Lorelai had become an entertainer; a stripper, to be blunt. One night, Lorelai asked me to join her as she went to pick up some of her things from work. Upon our arrival, her boss told her that he was 'low on girls.' I was content with just hanging at the bar, and although I was under aged, her boss was all right with me being there as well. She never thought I would do anything, but while she was working her shift, I was convinced to give the job a whirl. She walked into the back room of the club to find me all in hook, line and sinker. She may have been upset, but I was sold. In my mind, it beat working at Publix, a local grocery store, for pennies and restrictions. This form of "entertainment" became my new career of choice, up until the age of twenty-three.

I wish I could say that it was the depravity of the industry that convinced me to get out, but my father's death is what prompted me. His death changed me mentally. I realized that not one person in this world was going to help me and that if I wanted anything in this life; I had to be willing to do the very hard work it was going to take. Although I wish my father was still alive, I realize that it was his Last Will and Testament that snapped me out of the unconsciousness of my existence.

10

A Glimpse of Hope

*G*rowing up in the United States, my darkest hours were still illuminated by the sun. While my corner of the world once felt so small, it was looking through the portal of the Internet (however unreliable) that opened my eyes to the depravity that exists beyond my mere existence. Reflecting over the balance between what is real for me, and how my culture has influenced me, I can't help but realize that I was brainwashed into thinking there was some cookie cutter reality where I could find a blissful life filled with love, acceptance, and a place to fit in. I expected this would somehow come all wrapped up in a complete package—one filled with perfection, as there would be no more hardships, and every day would be filled with rainbows and butterflies. Laughter would be my hero, and love would never sting. My *Brady Bunch* mentality directed my footsteps, even if it was shoved deep down within my soul, creating a world of unmet expectations. The succession of disappointment after disappointment left me continually crushed.

Although I would never minimize the depth of my life experiences, my self-preserving Western vantage point always left me with some small glimpse of hope for a better life...

however unrealistic. That fight I felt within my heart may have been a dim flickering light, but it was there. I know this from the depths of my soul because my reality never truly offered me a reason to live; and yet, here I am. Movies and music were my therapy, as I would escape into alternate realities that taught me there was more to life than what was in front of me. Those fairytales penetrated my heart in profound ways. They gave me something to hold onto while I felt like I was continually falling deeper into the darkness of this world.

My life, up to the age of twenty-three, was clouded. There were many days I wanted to take my life. However, the zeal within me, encouraged by fictional stories that provided me with hope, saved me from ever following through. I lack the words to describe how, when I was depressed or lost in despair, all I saw was darkness . . . a void. I hid it well enough with drugs and the party life. However, at that point in my life, there was no concrete possibility of reaching through to the stronghold on my mindset.

I can finally see how the hand of God was always holding my heart. He spoke to my heart through the outlets that spoke to me, music and the movies. He cradled my heart as if it was His first love, never letting me slip away. It is the only explanation for why I never took my life. If God didn't have a plan for my life, the darkness I felt would have consumed me to ashes. I used to ask the question, "Why me? How can the guy or girl next door that did take that finalizing step of leaving this life no longer be here if I am?" I saw my life, and it was no more worthy than theirs. I realize that I may never fully understand until I stand in glory, but for now, I believe it might be so I could expose the darkness with the light that has brought me through to the other side, out of the depths of mental anguish.[2]

AWAKEN

When I was twenty-three years of age, the death of my father woke me up from my slumber in a way similar to being awakened after a terrifying nightmare; only my worst nightmare had come true. The impact felt like a baseball smacking me in the face, as I realized it was "do or die." What would I do next? It was by the grace of God I took the hardest step of my journey, one towards life.

His death came about six months after I moved back from North Carolina. I had already left Eric and was living with a fellow dancer. She was a girl that I connected with, and for some time, we were pretty tight. Through her, I connected with people that I went to middle school with, and we were having so much fun. However, I began to have a conscience regarding the things I was doing as my focus began to shift more towards family than the party life. I was still bugged out by people, but in my heart, I had an undeniable urge to spend time with my father. He and I were growing close because of those feelings. We were talking. Talking about anything and everything, and he was no longer making me feel like I was less than the choices I had made. We wanted to be in each others' lives. He was gently guiding me towards therapy so that we could begin the journey of restoration. I was still dancing, and my steps towards a healthy lifestyle were happening slowly, but I was putting one foot in front of the other during those six months. He saw that I was trying, and it was a very special time, one that I will cherish to my grave.

The day my father passed from this earth is as clear to me today as the very moment it happened. The weather outside was perfect, so I spent the day at Hollywood Beach, Florida with several of my friends. I can still feel the warmth on my face from the sun. I had butterflies as the feeling of fulfillment came over me for the first time since my childhood. I had real hope for my future as I sat looking out over the water. Something was speaking to my heart in a new way, and I knew things were about to change. I was craving the normalcy that began to seep into my thoughts and reality.

That evening, my father and I were going to have dinner, but he called to cancel because he was not feeling well. I didn't think anything of it as I wished him well. My friend, whom I was temporarily staying with, and I decided to go out instead. Those plans got spoiled as we were heading to leave.

It was 1997, and cell phones were not yet commonplace. Most people still used beepers, but my friend had a cell already. My mother had her number and called as we were sitting in the car plotting out our evening. A sunken feeling came over me immediately, as she appeared to turn slowly to look at me. I think time altered because everything just slowed down as I uttered, "My father has passed away, hasn't he?" Her face had a look of shock as she replied, "You don't know that; we only know he is in the hospital." I did know it, though. I knew he was gone, because less than five minutes before her phone rang, I experienced something that justified my thinking.

When my friend and I first sat in the car, I made a complete fool of myself. I saw a shadow in the doorway that sent chills spiraling throughout my whole body. It scared me to such a degree that the words leaped out of my mouth, "There is a spirit next to you." My friend looked at me like I was on drugs, but there you have it. I was sober, and I was not seeing things.

Another peculiar thing occurred as my friend was trying to console me on the way to the hospital. I felt his presence come over me; as if my father was physically there apologizing for everything he was responsible for that led me down such a harsh path. It is hard to put what I sensed into words, but it was as if he was telling me that he would have done it all differently if he had the opportunity. I had a real sensation of him apologizing to me. I believe it was that experience that gave me the strength that I needed to proceed, instead of sliding backward. I could have—should have—withered away; but I know even if it wasn't my father that I saw, it was something supernatural that brought me a message of hope, forgiveness, and the strength to carry on.

I could not fully comprehend everything I was feeling regarding the whole situation. The night of my father's death, I thought that life was playing a horrible joke on me. We had only a few great months together and just as we were turning the corner... he was taken from me. I was never able to show him that I was sorry for my actions and barely told him by my words. This made the pain I felt stab me ever so deeply. I believe it is one of those things I will carry with me until the day I leave this life, like a permanent scar.

As I was sitting in shock at the hospital, having just seen my father lying lifeless, my brother walked in. I began to cry, and my stomach felt like it was dropping to my feet. We did not spend much time at the hospital after his arrival. After all, there was no real need to be there any longer. We went back to my father's house, and my ideals of what a family should be versus my reality collided head-on that evening. Life had most undoubtedly changed for everyone involved, including my father's girlfriend who had lived with him.

Having just had a birthday the day before, my brother went from a young, carefree college graduate who was just starting his life, to stepping into the role of his deceased father. He surely must have been dying inside; he just lost his best friend. I wanted nothing more than to have a healthy outlook on life at that moment so that I could have been his deepest comfort. However, I was the strange and foreign sister who ran away and, as his father was going through some awkward transitions himself, happened to be present again. Needless to say, we did not spend 'us' time together as most families would do, with no distractions. We did not send anyone away, so we could just have a moment to process together the passing of our father. We did not grow close due to this horrific circumstance. We didn't pause to finally get to know each other, or cry in one another's arms, or help each other deal with the trauma. We just passed the evening together as strangers, who happened to be in the same boat during a storm.

A TIME TO MOURN

Following my father's funeral, my brother and I "sat Shiva" at my father's house together. This is a seven-day mourning period in the Jewish religion, and friends and family come bearing lots and lots of food. It was very strange to be sleeping in my old bed once again. It felt like I was in a parallel universe: there was all the same furniture, but a different perspective.

The second night of sitting Shiva I was seated in the family room. We had an awesome couch that was in the shape of the letter U. I was positioned in a way that, as it was getting dark outside I could still make out all the young adults sitting out by the pool area. The stark differences between my brother and I became clear to me for the first time in my life. I knew that leaving home and all that I had seen and done were on the opposite side of the coin from the suburban normality of Pleasantville. The difference between every person that graced our front door and me was painfully obvious. Jealousy began to rise within me like I had never felt before. The guilt that consumed my whole being became overshadowing, and it took every ounce of strength I had not to get up and run. It was only by the grace of God that I took all that I was feeling and sought to find some form of solace. I had to work at fitting in without being problematic. I found amongst my brother's friends those who were fun and carefree, and I plugged right in. I grabbed onto every stupid joke and every unsure smile that I received and sought to be what I believed they wanted me to be. I think that was when my acting skills came into play. My father always said I would have made a great actress.

I was a wild child who barely knew how to relate to people, an abused little girl slowly trying to pull herself out of the trash can she lived in. Anyone with open eyes could have seen that I just needed to know that I was wanted and loved. My family, at that time, could not see through the surface of my past. I was there with an open heart, just wanting to be let back in.

During the week we sat Shiva, the people around me seemed to have lacked the comprehension of what drove the little girl in me down such a dirty path, and the neglect of parents that kept her there. Feeling like a complete waste of space, even if I was making positive steps before my father's passing, all I wanted in my heart was my family. However, I had to learn that some people in this life choose to wrong others instead of recognizing that we all live in a fallen world filled with brokenness. Those types of people, when given an opportunity to embrace forgiveness in order to produce healthy growth, miss the mark and cause further damage. That is what happened to me, but I share this with forgiveness in my heart, knowing that each and every one of us operates within our own limitations. At that time though, I was finally bonding with my father and pulling my life together one baby step at a time. After sitting Shiva, any ounce of belief within me that was rooted in thinking that I was loved or wanted, was crushed. Instead, I was left with a hole in my heart that fed my insecurities.

Ultimately, the week did do something positive for me, as it caused me to desire genuinely to return to the land of the living instead of running away from it. The following week, I cleaned out my locker at work and said my goodbyes. The other girls were all very supportive of me; hugging me tightly, speaking words of encouragement, and even presenting me with a card full of money. I thought to myself as I was leaving that day that I would return and help make a difference in the lives of the girls who find themselves slaves to such depravity. I would work hard so that I would be able to teach others that there were favorable opportunities for them, too. Even though I was not then where I am today, it is a blessing to see how God still gave me small nuggets that pointed me toward my future.

A NEW PATH

A new path emerged after the passing of my father. As I turned the corner to begin walking down that path, it was the start of a new semester. I moved into my new apartment that my father had helped me find. One of my childhood friends moved in with me, and I even put myself into therapy, attending the free counseling sessions that the school offered. My brother honored my father's monetary wishes toward me for the first semester of college, and that is how I was able to transition financially into my new path without my father.

I had attended and finished some classes here and there throughout my dark phase, but it was not until after my father passed that I tucked away all my fears, and jumped in full swing. Hunger within me rose above my insecurities. I found strength through my pain and anger instead of ignoring them with drugs. I began to channel all my feelings, emotions, and thoughts toward a desire to prove to a world that did not believe in me that it could not hold me down. The desire stemmed from the day I read, "To my daughter, good luck in life." The will of my father that was put into place had me left out. The irony is that my father told me a week before his passing that he had fixed his will. He said that he had put me back in it, so that I would be well taken care of, and that he loved me and was so excited for the future. However, my family believed at the time that I should fully experience the consequences of my childhood choices.

Upon reading those seven words, I did not even hand the booklet back to the clerk. I just ran out of the courthouse with tears streaming down my face. As I was leaving, I began the recitation in my mind, "He never wanted me! He never loved me or cared, and this proves it. Everyone will see, I will show them that I can make it without family." I dwelt on those words for the next five years of my life, and the fight to prove myself is really what got me through.

That rejection created a readiness to move forward, and nothing was going to get in my way. Something truly snapped inside of me, and that is why, when my brother offered to pay for my school, I went happily. After the first semester, he took back that offer, though. I had a few C's on my report card, and he told me he wasn't going to pay for my classes if I wasn't going to try. Little did he know, I was trying as hard as I possibly could. Had he understood all sides that influenced my past, he would have seen that I was absolutely putting everything I had into school. In my eyes, those C's were A's because I did not even know how to study, let alone read and write on par with those around me. Passing my classes, to me, was a huge leap forward. I did not allow his choice to stop me; it only drove me to work harder. I got a job working at the school and took out student loans. Five years later, I graduated with a Bachelor's Degree in Computer Information Systems from Florida Atlantic University.

HE LOOKED NORMAL . . .

A few weeks before my father passed away, I met my third serious relationship. I was still dancing, and despite his hidden issues, he eventually became my whole world. I was very intimidated by him when we first met. Michael was this tall, dark, and handsome man who looked like he could be in the movies. He was established in so many ways. For instance, he owned his own business. He had it together, at least, compared to what I was used to. He even had lots of family and friends around him at all times, and for some reason, he took a strong liking towards me, even though I was a roaring mess.

The death of my father, I believe, played a major part in my attachment to him. He was the first person that actually showed me any form of proper attention. He would take me on dates, and we would talk on the phone until all hours of the night. He even loved taking me shopping. That was something I had to get used to, but let's face it, that didn't take long. When he bought me my first cell phone, I was so taken back. He had to encourage me to accept it from him. It was a monumental transition from my past, which involved two guys that beat me up physically or emotionally abused me, to dating one who clearly was not going to do either.

When my mother first met him, she hilariously embarrassed me by the way she shared her approval of him in every way. The day they met, I had asked Michael to help my mother and me pick up a truck from Eric's home. The moment she saw

Michael, not knowing that we were dating, her first words to me were, "Now, why can't you meet a guy like this?" We all started to laugh, and the rest is history.

We officially began dating within the same week my father passed away, and he was there for me through my period of grieving. During our first year together, I was living in the apartment my father got me, and we were developing what seemed like a genuine relationship. In my eyes, I started to believe he was everything that I deserved. He helped me financially and encouraged me to not fall back into dancing. We did things together that seemed so normal, like going to the fair. I even had a well-balanced lifestyle between school, other friends, and time with him. Life began to blossom as I started to trust myself to have healthy relationships.

Things changed for us a little over a year of being together. I ended up getting pregnant, which tore me up inside. My fears and feelings of my past came rushing forward, and I became angry with myself for allowing this to happen. I knew this time that I wanted to keep my child. I had always just wanted a family. In many ways, when I was with Josh, I had allowed myself to get pregnant, so I could have someone to love that would love me back. In this instance, however, I didn't do that and I was not going to repeat what I did in my past.

As I sat in Michael's house sharing the news with him, he made it very clear that he was not open to the idea of keeping the child. I cried, and I begged him, but there was no budging. In those days, I had no conscience that there was someone else's life inside of me. I just thought, "Oh, in the first three months it is safe to abort." I lacked education and so putting my relationship with Michael above understanding, I respected his wishes, and I found myself having an abortion. It changed our relationship, though. Once again, my past became my filter, and the newness of our relationship wore off. He felt it too, and it was not long afterward that I learned that he was keeping a dark secret from me. It came out that he had a tremendous addiction to crack cocaine. That is the worst form of cocaine that anyone could use. When I learned this, I should have run far away. Deep down, I knew I should have. I did take a few months away from him thinking that I would not go back. I was still in my early 20s and on what seemed like the right path. However, it was not long before the malignant attachment that grew within my heart had me back at his house, fighting for us to be together again.

I believed that he was worth fighting for. Clouded by the pain from all my choices that lead up to that point, and the subconscious sorrow I felt towards the loss of all my children, I ended up in a very unhealthy way pouring all my energy into trying to fix Michael. He was not that into me trying either, and it created a very rocky relationship that ended up sucking the life right out of me.

THE BLIND LEADING THE BLIND

A drug user trying to help an addict is as insane as a person playing with matches and gasoline simultaneously. We went back and forth between him not wanting me, me not wanting him, him fighting for me, me fighting for him. We were just two genuinely hurting people, who wanted to be free of all the nonsense. We just did not know how to get free.

Like myself, he too had a harsh upbringing. His mother passed away when he was young, leaving him in the care of his older siblings. Most of them were already severe drug users, so their influence on him was destructive. His father was in prison most of his life and happened to get out while we were still together. When I think of Michael, I think of a wonderful human being who had all the potential in the world. He was not only good looking, but also smart, ambitious, and a caring young man who would give the shirt off his back to anyone who needed it.

The shackles of addiction and the power of a dysfunctional family can keep the most vibrant and extraordinary of people from ever achieving their full capabilities. They are left only to sample in small doses the light that wants to shine, while the drugs and disillusionment push the potential down further and further. The end result is usually a life lived through depression, confusion, and ultimately brokenness.

Despite it all, we both deeply loved one another and tried many things to boost our relationship. We went to church, even though we didn't believe in our hearts. We went to some hippie self-help program called Landmark Education. We talked deeply with one another and even considered moving far away. However, by the time I graduated college, I was drained to the point that I had nothing left in me to give to another human being. After five years of giving every ounce of myself to fighting for breakthroughs, I had nothing left inside me but a drained and broken spirit.

In my worldview, graduating college meant that I could accomplish something positive in my life. I had left the heavy drugs behind for the most part, but he was not showing any sign that he would ever break the addiction. Leaving him once and for all was like losing my father all over again, as I broke away from the only person that I felt genuinely loved me. It did not help that he called me practically every day for the first six months after I left. I did not pick up the phone until I knew I could handle it, but ultimately it took years for me to heal from that relationship. I have had only one, short-term relationship since him.

Two years after Michael and I broke up, I met a young man that I had gone to college with. He was as straight-laced as they come, and we became a couple not long after we met. I tried to love him. I saw the possibility of a healthy relationship with him, but no matter how much I tried, I could never give him my heart, it was too damaged.

He was a young man who came from an Orthodox Jewish family. It was during my relationship with him that I spent a whole year without any drugs in my system. It was bizarre and extremely difficult having to deal with all my emotions and thoughts. To this day, I feel bad for him receiving the brunt of that hardship. I do not know why he even chose to put up with me for as long as he did.

Trying to remain sober at all times, I found that there was no heart left in me, no trust left in me, and no logic to help me reason. He tried, though. He did his best to help me experience a healthy life, but in the end, he was not going to win me over.

A STEP FORWARD

I believe the young Jewish guy was a stepping-stone because I relearned how to care for myself through that relationship. Yet, after I broke up with him, I partied once again and dated a few people who were friends with my brother. That opened the door for my brother and me to start talking again. Those two guys were not serious relationships at all, but it was through those experiences that I realized how damaged I truly was. My eyes were slowly opening, and I eventually pulled away once and for all from everyone and everything.

It was New Year's Eve the day I realized that I did not want any part of the life that I was living. I was thirty-one. I had dropped ecstasy, and while customarily that drug made me feel pure happiness, this evening I felt disconnected with the world around me. That was something that drugs typically did not do to me. I used them so I could feel connected with ease, without any of my fortress-sized walls around me. That particular evening, something inside me clicked as I looked around at the room full of people and thought, "There is nothing that I will ever find here that will fill me up." After seventeen years of all the wrong choices filled with so much pain and suffering, it dawned on me that as long as I stayed where I was, I would never experience anything but what I had. Cycles can come in so many different shapes and sizes wrapped with different packaging, but in the end, I realized that I was the common denominator that needed to be removed.

It was at this time that I reached out to my brother, and we started the process towards a wholesome friendship. It would take ten more years for it to finally flourish, but during those days, I would visit him as often as I could. He was living in Miami, where I worked, so it was easy to spend time with him. He even came to visit me a couple of times at my condo in Sunrise. It was a genuine and unconditional relationship forming between us. He even agreed to loan me $10,000 to purchase an investment property. However, he was unsettled about the loan, as he made clear through a few emails. Who could blame him? Nevertheless, I paid him back in full within a year. That taught him that he could trust me, at least to some degree. We even had a few things in common, namely computers and video games, and those interests helped us grow in our relationship.

It seemed like yesterday when he introduced me to what would become yet another addiction of mine. Thankfully, this one didn't involve drugs. He sat me down at his computer and introduced me to the game World of Warcraft. I fell head over heels in love with this game, and it provided me with enough distraction to keep away from the party life, including all my friends. For two whole years, I was sucked in like a piece of paper in a tailpipe, flapping in the wind on a moving car. It was the strangest of times for me, as I connected with people from all over the world in the most alarming way. We "gamers" treated this game as if it was crucially important. The nonsense that happened in that game is a book in and of itself.

Although I admit that it was an unhealthy addiction, that video game changed my life. It gave me an outlet to get safely sober while engaging with other people virtually. God used that outlet; I believe because it was there, in my sober and lost state of mind, that God met me. Three good things came out of the countless hours I spent in that virtual world. One was my brother, as we were able to connect through our little characters running around in *Azeroth*. Second, I made a few friends that have become a part of my life, and third, I came to faith in Jesus.

11

ACCEPTANCE

....

At the age of fourteen, I ran away from arms that did not try to hold me back, searching for something real, something that would fix the pain of rejection I felt, and for a place where I knew I was loved. Consumed by an altered perception of what was real, I ran and kept running consistently into my adult life. Everything failed no matter how much I tried to be what others needed. Like Humpty Dumpty, I failed to find anyone that could put me back together again. There were no magic pills, perfect self-help systems, or legalistic religious paths that could make me whole again. Getting the right job, making real money, having the right body mass, eating the right foods, having a good therapist, and having all the right girlfriends could have contributed to a full life; yet there was nothing in any of those things that could help me clear my mind.

A life lived on the surface, stuffing down all that had happened to me and all that I had done, could not cut it for me. I felt broken, as depression plagued my sober thoughts, prodding me to keep me looking for that next high. Every single attempt I made in life was lacking because the thing that mattered most, finding acceptance, failed me over and over and I washed all the pain away through drug use. I had some misconstrued belief that if I found the one man who was strong enough, stable enough, and able to love me, I would heal and become the healthy woman I knew I could be. At the end of the day, however, people came and went, things were new and old, and there I was, always left with myself, no matter how perfect my life looked on the outside because of my achievements.

At the age of thirty-one, I had overcome so much and had achieved more than I ever thought possible. I had life in the palm of my hands. Surprisingly, the buffet of life set before me proved to be empty and meaningless, and my eyes turned toward the only thing that would ever be able to fill me up. I looked up and saw the only place where I would be able to come as broken as I was without trying to fix myself. A place where the focus would eventually shift from inward toward something greater than myself. A place where what I tasted was an everlasting flavor that ran deeper than anything I had experienced so far in this life. That place was in the arms of my Maker, the One who fashioned me before the foundation of this earth. The One that, in a fallen world where all I could see was tainted by pain and suffering, had never forgotten me. His love, mercy, and grace are more than any one human being will need to get by in this world. It has always been right there, ready for me to experience it. It was a gift that was free, but the way of righteousness is a truly narrow and hard path to take.[3]

It meant first believing in something that is supernatural and difficult to believe in, especially with all the doubt that clogged my mind. My closest companion was fear, and she was leading me over and above trust. How could I trust anyone? Wasn't it God who allowed me to go through all that I had been through in the first place? I was angry at God. Even so, my eyes were opened to see the last person on earth I would've expected. After all, I am Jewish!

JESUS, WHO?

The day that I uttered the words, "God forgive me for how I have lived my life, forgive me of my sins. I accept that Jesus is the Messiah, so please draw me close to you," I felt as small as an ant, sitting in that church. The pastor was giving a message based on the expression "all roads lead to Rome," and how it had lost its credibility beyond the gates of the Roman era. To prove his point to an audience sitting in Fort Lauderdale, Florida, he stated to us that we can't say, "all roads lead to Orlando" because we can't drive towards Miami to get to Orlando. Furthermore, we can't get to Rome without an airplane or boat. His point was that many people use that expression to indicate that all beliefs lead to heaven. Nevertheless, God made it very clear in Scripture that He designed only one path to lead to Him. Jesus, during His last Passover meal with his disciples, explained to the twelve of them that because they believe in God, they should also believe in Him. Hearing the disciples were most concerned about being able to physically follow Him, He explained, "I am the way, and the truth, and the life; no one comes to the Father but through Me."[4]

Hearing the pastor say these things was a very hard pill for me to swallow. I began to contemplate that idea. If all paths did lead to God, then we could live our lives however we wanted to, without any sacrifice or consequences. It also dawned on me as I reflected on my life that we did live in a cause and effect world. I realized that the world already acknowledged this truth. Even if they didn't walk closely with God, they just called it Karma.

There I was, sitting in church that day, already believing

in the Scriptures as the word of God. I already had that presupposition going in. The thing was, I didn't like for Christians to use "their Bible" to prove a point to me, a Jewish girl. I needed to see it within the Hebrew Scriptures, so as I was listening to the Pastor and contemplating revelations concerning my life, I began talking to God. I told Him that there was no way that I would ever believe in Jesus unless He made it clear to me that He was the Messiah of Israel. In my heart, I believed the God of Israel was, and is, the only true God. My Jewish heritage meant the world to me then, and it still does. I began praying for a sign, and to my surprise, I received one. I looked toward the right of the stage, and I saw an Israeli flag. It did not just appear there, but I most certainly didn't notice it until that moment. I always had prided myself on how observant I was, but it goes to show that no matter how much we think we notice things, everyone has blind spots.

I was not looking to become a believer in Jesus. I was very aware of the treatment and history of so-called Christians and their mindset toward my people group. At that moment though, I can't put into words the comfort and peace that came over me. God found me and I believed. It is just what happened that day. A sense of confirmation came over me as I reflected back to when I was dating the young man from the Orthodox family. I had spent Yom Kippur with him and his family. It is the Day of Atonement, a day we fast and pray for the forgiveness of our sins that year. It was during that process in temple, that I had quietly prayed to God that I wanted to know Him, and to turn my life over to Him.

Nine years later, my walk with God is deep and wide, and the transformation that has happened in my life is undoubtedly due to His mighty work in it. It is not rooted in a denomination or religious people group, or the tainted history that stains their doorpost. One may judge me and put me into the box titled "Christian," a word that means all kinds of different things to different people. At the heart of the word "Christian," is Christ, the Greek word for Messiah. It means "a Christ follower" and that is what I am! Therefore, with all the history of dysfunction to the side, I find myself tapping into the only aspect that matters; that is, my relationship with God through my Messiah.

My bloodline didn't change just because I believe in Jesus. Therefore, I am in my heart still a Jewish girl, but my relationship with God has become the foundation of my life. It is through that relationship that I was transformed from who you have read about in these pages to a woman that outshines her past. When people look at me, they usually cannot wrap their mind around the fact that I have experienced even an ounce of my past. That brings me so much pleasure. In my eyes, that is the mighty power of God renewing one's mind when they surrender their life and everything they are holding onto to His will and ways.

12

LETTING GO

Somewhere among the weeds of my young life, I developed a co-dependent tendency. I became emotionally attached to how others perceived me. While it may have made my relationships interesting and fun, it most definitely kept me in a state of emotional upheaval. When I ran away, I ran because I wanted to find a place where I would be wanted. That was the root of my co-dependency; I lived in fear of being rejected. It consumed me like a fire. I knew, even in my turmoil, that something was not right. As I got older, blame was redirected from other people to myself. For that reason, I ended up wandering right into the bottomless pit of self-help propaganda.

While I was still dating Michael, we took a class together that grew out of Erhard Seminars Training known as EST, a self-improvement course that started in the 1960s. Landmark Education is the modern version of this course. It was in that class that I learned how to take the first step towards changing my pattern of thinking. The program has different techniques that they use to help people step out of their interpretation of their life. For instance, I had to write out my whole story up to that point, and read it to one other person, over and over again. This was executed while they played kindergarten music in the background. It was through this technique, as odd as it was that I realized for the first time that though I might have been a victim of my circumstances, I was now *choosing* to live life through a victim mentality. Understandably, I was coping with life through the eyes of my past. Growing up, I did learn how to survive in a harsh world, and that world defined my life experiences.

Although many of the things in my life had happened to me, this class challenged me to acknowledge that I too was responsible for my choices. My current theological underpinning might keep me from agreeing with the root teaching that defines Landmark's philosophy on life, but I am grateful for this experience, as it opened my mind to realize that there are more sides to "my story" than just my own. That simple truth dawned on me, and even though I had justifiable reasons for stumbling down the path I did, my actions had an adverse impact on my family. I too played a part in the great dysfunction that dominated us. My life was not all about me!

Somewhere along the line of hormonal adolescence, I put my mother on a pedestal of perfection. Perhaps it grew out of my desire to protect her when I was a child; in my mind, nothing she did was wrong. I would beat myself up for her actions, which made it very difficult to give her the space to be that which she is, human.

Landmark opened my eyes. I started to take her off that pedestal. I learned how to give my mom the space to make mistakes, without making her choices about me. We still had many years of fighting left between us, but gaining a new perspective of her enabled me to be more empathetic. I had to accept that my mother would never be the type of mom that I wanted. She was going to be exactly who she was, based on how she wanted to live her life. That was something very hard to accept, especially since I needed something that was very real from her that she simply could not give.

The journey of healing has not been a smooth ride. As a runaway, I have always known that I had to fight for what I wanted. It was the fight that caused me to go out into a scary world in the first place. There is nothing in this world that is worth having if it did not take tremendous dedication and effort to achieve. Who has genuinely appreciated something when it was just handed to them?

In this life, there is no such thing as drive-thru therapy that gives you your order of healing at the second window. I had to go to the store, buy the ingredients, prepare the dish, and cook it. I even had to clean up after eating and processing. It was quite a journey; it was ten years from the time I took Landmark until I finally started witnessing the fruit of emotional and mental freedom in my life. Six of those years were spent in biblical counseling, learning how to see my life through the eyes of what God says about me in His Word, and how to stop clinging to the fear of rejection like a monkey clings to a tree. That, my friend, is where the real healing happened!

When I first came to faith in 2005, I trembled in my skin in a world where I felt no freedom to share about who I was or where I came from. In my sober state, shame and fear fought against God's hand as I found myself in a foreign land known as "the Christian world." The vulnerable state I was in made it nearly impossible to engage with those around me. All those years that I never dealt with my emotions came crashing down on me like a tidal wave. I spent six years of my faith in and out of depression as different things came rushing forth. Despite all the obstacles that kept showing up through my efforts in this new Christian world, I was finally working through all the memories and emotions that I had shoved deep down. They were coming up as if I had emotional food poisoning.

Every day of the first six to seven years of my faith, I lived with a fear similar to public speaking. Even though I was in isolation from people, I still felt fear. It was at that time that I learned to look to God and to put something that is not physically tangible above all my life experiences. These were experiences that created survival skills out of circumstances that were at times real and my feelings were rightly felt and at other times the interpretation of a young child that constructed ideas of what she thought was happening to her. Whether my feelings were based on fact or fiction, after six years of hard, sober work through biblical counseling, I finally came to the conclusion that I needed to loosen up. I was extremely hard on myself. Thanks to my dedicated counselor in New York City, I learned how to validate my feelings when they were difficult for me to process. She taught me how just to stop and acknowledge, "Hey, so this is what rejection feels like."

I became aware of how to process my emotions to such a degree that I was no longer stuffing them away or standing in the confusion of what I was feeling. I was learning how to be healthy in terms of handling the life that was now around me, so I began acknowledging the sensations that went along with my emotions. It cracked open a door into a world of emotional freedom where co-dependency became recognizable and controllable.

There were some other things that I had to work out alongside my emotions; survival skills had placed a filter over my eyes. I saw the world through different patterns of thought, which predetermined my perceptions. It all boiled down to this: I needed to break my pattern of thinking so I could make room for God to start His process of transformation. My boss in New

York City became a tremendous pillar in my life through this acknowledgment. She became the disciplinary mother that I desperately needed as she spoke into my life with such truth in a loving way. She noticed within my eyes a woman who was trying to break free from the chains of her past, and she gave me the chance to blossom. That is all I needed; someone who would believe in me and prove to me that I was not going to be rejected just because I made mistakes. I was struggling to become who I was designed to be because I believed lies about who I really am. She identified that struggle, so she guided me toward the path that would help me see truth versus lies.

Einstein stated this in the best way, "Everybody is a genius. But if you judge a fish by its ability to climb a tree, it will live its whole life believing that it is stupid." She saw who I was even when others could not, despite the fact that I did not know how to walk in truth. I was accustomed to walking in the lies that I believed about myself. Therefore, I was left with the only thing that would help me have a breakthrough. I perceived, through her coaching, that I had patterns of thinking that were getting in the way of seeing things for what they truly were. I needed to discard the old filter of my past, and replace it with a brand new one.

For instance, when I saw things negatively, I learned to go to prayer with my perception instead of declaring in my mind a fixed fate for the circumstance. Through this process, I have learned to stop fighting myself by trusting in something greater than me: God. This has allowed me to give people and things all the space they need to be who they are while creating very healthy boundaries in my life.

Although I have learned how to utilize biblical tools to help me process life in a sober way so that my deepest fear of rejection no longer controls me, there are times still that I'm guilty of putting my mom back into my box of expectations. The difference today is that standing on what has become my Cornerstone, I've been able to cut the umbilical cord. I have learned to seek God daily for my fulfillment in life, and because of that daily choice, I've been able to discover mental and emotional freedom from the needs of my younger self. I've learned that creating boundaries and keeping my mother in perspective has given me the skill set to keep my expectations out of our relationship. We have finally come to a place where we both acknowledge the love that exists from the unfailing bond between a mother and daughter. That love at times is all we have keeping us in each others' lives. We have also learned through many rough patches that at the heart of our struggle lies the need for respect. Our similarities indeed overshadow the fact that we both look into the lens of life ever so differently. I have come to the realization that each day is a gift with her. It is by the strength that I have found in my walk with God that I can operate in a state of peace with her. I truly cherish the good moments, while I no longer fight her during the hard ones.

These truths extend to my brother, and even to my father who is not here to receive it. When I was 26 years old and in the midst of the Landmark course, I picked up the phone despite how nervous I was, and I was nervous. Just four years before, while we were sitting Shiva, I became strangely intimidated by my brother and frightened to be myself around him. Fear, however, was never something that kept me from moving forward, so I called him for the first time in years. At that moment, I authentically acknowledged how running away had hurt him, that I loved him, and that I was very sorry. He told me that he appreciated my phone call, but that he created a family for himself through friends. He was open, though, as he continued to tell me that he was willing to let me prove myself in time. At the moment, I did not feel disappointment that I didn't get an instant acceptance. The mere fact that he took my phone call brought me a sigh of relief. I appreciated his honesty. Obtaining his trust, love, and friendship became my focus pertaining to our relationship. As I acknowledged what I did, it honestly did not matter about the things I knew he had done. He was more important than his actions. Just like God feels about His creation, for we are all fallen creatures, but He loves us more than our depravity.

My brother meant those words to me on the phone that day long ago, for our relationship had started to flourish by the time I was thirty years old. I realized that truth when he came to celebrate my birthday with me, and I could not have asked for a better gift. Then, not even a couple years later when I came to faith in Jesus, he became unconditionally accepting of me. He opened up his home, and I moved in with him for a few months as I prepared to leave South Florida.

I originally moved to North Carolina, but after three years, a door opened for me to move to New York City. My brother encouraged me, and he would say things like, "I may not believe in Jesus, but I am so proud of the growth I see in you." He told me also that it was my strength that encouraged him to want to make the changes he had made in his life. It was very clear that he looked up to me as a person who overcame adversity. We still had a few more rough patches, but today we have finally arrived at a place of unconditional love and acceptance.

13

FOR MY CHILDREN

··

Sitting on a park bench overlooking the lake, the stillness in the air was not from the climate but from the peace that was coming over me as I felt my darkest secret being exposed. The healing that seemed like a lifetime to obtain, yet would be only a few months, was summed up in that very moment. You could hear a pin drop as the trees softly swayed and a man on his kayak floated by on the calmness of the water. Leading up to that very intimate moment, I had been living in North Carolina already for two years. I had come to taste the freedom from the chains that held me down, but a cloud of sorrow followed me day in and day out. In fear of man, I operated my life closed off from those around me, never wanting to allow others to see my dark spots. With only one foot in the different communities I engaged, I tried my best to connect.

There were a few people from each community that trickled into my life, who I grew to feel comfortable around. Most of those people have become family to me, and as I shared bits and pieces of my past with them, they were genuinely helpful as I wrestled with healing. Some were sheltered but had a tremendous gift of compassion; others had life experiences outside of the bubble that the Christian world creates within their communities. No matter their history, those select few made such a tremendous impact on my life, and I praise God for them each and every day.

I was working on my Master of Divinity in Biblical Counseling, which became my best friend. I drowned myself in the books and the homework assignments. I focused on keeping my eyes on the prize of growing closer to my God. I had moved to North Carolina to learn more about my faith, and my depression pushed me to dig deeper into my soul. I wanted to heal so much that I could taste it.

The ability to have breakthroughs did not come without hard work, patience, and lots and lots of prayer. There were many days that I was crying out for help in silence. The once outspoken loud mouth was now timid and fearful because I felt out of place most days. It was a real struggle to connect with those around me. I pushed myself to be open, and because of that, I was blessed to meet two very different couples. They became instrumental in my growth just because they showed that they cared. For me!

One was an older couple with children close in age to me. They first noticed me sitting in church one day. It was from that moment on that they became nurturing parents that spoke into my life, providing me the disciplinary guidance that I needed to feel encouraged in the path God was taking me down.

The second couple was a Jewish family who believed in Yeshua, Jesus, just like I do. They were second generation believers, and were very solid, emotionally and spiritually. They played a big part in my life because they also noticed me and chose to invest in my well-being. To this day, both couples play an impactful role in my life, and I will cherish them forever.

Through those few but intense years, because of those relationships, I learned that I was lovable and worth being desired, as a friend and family member. They say "blood is thicker than water" is an analogy for the bond of family, but that is not always the case. Sometimes it is the people who are in your life that are not blood-related that draw you out and help you see your self-worth above and beyond the impact made in one's life by blood family. That type of friendship is true commitment and unbreakable.

It was during my time with these unique people, and the intensity of my Biblical counseling classes, where I learned that I was living my life with a guilt padded with pain, and it ruled my heart and mind. I believed in the truth that God had rescued me from the penalty of sin, but wondered how could someone who has done the things that I have done deserve to be forgiven? I was still punishing myself for my choices, because the shame that consumed me was real, and it kept me from drawing deeper into my relationships… kept me from actually living. I could no longer hide from it all through the use of drugs. I had to deal with everything head on. As I stumbled around in the foreign land I was in; God held my hand as He brought me to my knees, revealing to me how to work through every choice one by one.

The thing that haunted me the most was the death of my children. Through the guidance of one of my professors, I found myself at the doorsteps of the Pregnancy Support Services Center. I wanted to put a bag over my head as I got out of my car to go inside. I wasn't walking in because of one abortion, but because of four. Six children passed through my body. Two were taken from me during my marriage, but the other four lost their lives due to the choices of a lost and confused young girl. I did not understand my past then like I do today, so the feeling of being a scumbag never felt as alive within my skin as it did at that moment.

My children never got to breathe the fresh air of life outside of my womb. They never got to grow up and experience the roller coaster of experiences that would have formed them into who they would have been. They never got to smell a flower or taste ice cream. They never got to get mad at me and storm away. Who was I to desire anything good in this life when I was a murderer? I chose to terminate their lives when they had no say in the matter, because of my own selfish reasoning.

The one thing I have craved the most throughout my journey has been family. The desire for one has been my biggest thorn in the flesh. Thus, my imagination would dream of what life would have been like had I given birth to at least one of them. The pregnancy center taught me, however, to not dwell on *the could haves and would haves,* but to focus on the reality that it was not up to me to do the forgiving for my past. Through that process, I wrote a letter to each of my children and even gave them names. It might seem a bit morbid, but it helped me recognize them, so I could work out the condemnation that kept me locked in the box of wrongdoing.

God brought me through the heavy counseling that I needed in order to heal from those choices. I believe there will always be a scar that has their names on it. However, the day I sat at a picnic table overlooking a lake with a couple of my closest girlfriends and my counselor, holding the names of my children, some meaningful Bible verses, and breathing lots and lots of prayer, a cloud of darkness rose up and away from hovering over my life.

As we sat there in silence after I spoke out each of their names and prayed for them to forgive me, it was as if there was a door that opened up from heaven. With the sun blazing and not a cloud in the sky, it started to sprinkle on us! We all busted out in laughter with the sense of God baptizing the moment.

The air of forgiveness spoke volumes into the moment as our laughter turned into joyful tears. We all realized that, just like we saw countless times in Scripture, once a person was healed from their physical sickness, they were spiritually cleansed by the washing of water. My choices will always be a part of my life, but God washed me clean of my abortions. I felt it, as did the witnesses around me. The condemnation was gone, as I was no longer defined in my mind by who I once was and the choices I made, but by who I am and the choices I will make. For that, I give God all the glory!

14

CLOSURE

A‌cknowledging our part in any circumstance is difficult, especially when our culture teaches us it is alright to point the finger at others. Realizing that forgiveness, both for others and from others, is a significant aspect of healing, has been key to my freedom. In my life, without forgiveness, co-dependency would win . . . leaving me in a mental and emotional struggle. Forgiveness was hard for me, especially when the feeling of condemnation was plastered all over the walls of my mind. The internal struggle between walking out forgiveness and wanting to defend myself had been like a nervous tick that would not go away. However, I learned the difference between condemnation and constructive criticism. While one places you in a box and seals it up, the latter points out the obvious to draw out the light within. I have also learned that when someone, including myself, wants to hold me back through condemnation, it is because of fear of looking inward. This truth has helped me in the journey of being set free from the opinions of others, my insecurities, and ultimately to have forgiveness toward people even when they have not asked for it.

As I have learned to revisit my life with the word of God

as my guide to understanding it in all its facets, I discovered several things about myself. I realized that I'd been lost within the pride of holding onto having to be right, how I perceived others, and ultimately, the fear of losing control. I realized that I had to let go of those things by accepting my faults instead of pointing the finger. That did not mean I took the blame for everything, but I realized that no one is perfect and that the world, despite its mistakes, is not out to get me. I was only able to begin grasping the true meaning of forgiveness once my heart was open to realizing how forgiven I am by God through my faith in Jesus.

I was once told, "those who are greatly forgiven are those who know how to forgive greatly." Believing as I do about God taught me that we live in a broken world where dysfunction influences the heart of mankind. The story of redemption is a reality, one in which the broken can turn their heart over to the Great Physician. He releases the chains of sin and death by his unfailing power through the blood of our sacrificial lamb. Through this reality I have learned what true forgiveness is, a forgiveness that meant that whatever the circumstance I was in, it no longer had to linger in my heart. I could choose God over and beyond the burden, which tried to grab a hold of my thoughts.

Although I believe that the power of condemnation is rendered powerless as I walk by faith, I still have had to do the hard work of choosing to seek God daily for the guidance and strength to perceive and engage this world. There is truly no cookie cutter technique. For me, though, personal acceptance, daily prayer, scripture reading, and turning from how I used to live my life has brought about real transformation. A transformation that has taught me the difference between joy in my heart and the happiness I initially set out to find when I was fourteen.

When I was a little girl riding in the car with my family, I would stare out the window dreaming of a better life. As we passed communities that I thought were "poor" neighborhoods, I would ignorantly think, "That is where happiness is." I learned the hard way that being financially poor is not where one finds happiness, either. In my adult life, as I was learning how to identify my emotions that tied to different feelings, I realized that happiness is just that, a feeling—a sensation. It has no substance; it is just a stimulate response to something. Ironically, many people say the phrase, "If you are happy that is all that matters." Feelings come and go. Every day brings new experiences and circumstances both in and out of my control, so even though I have discovered a place of peace, happiness cycles in and out of my life.

My faith has taught me that a godly joy is what I want, not a feeling that passes through me like a wave hitting the seashore. I desire a joy that exists within all circumstances good or bad, and I can say with a full heart that I found that within my relationship with God.[5] I am in agreement with Heraclitus, an ancient Greek philosopher, "the only thing constant is change itself." Therefore, it should not matter what I feel because I am guaranteed to feel all the emotions that humans experience. Trust me when I say that, as a stereotypical New York Jewish girl, I move through the list of feelings easily. However, as long as I focus on God and His hope for me, I can rest in the joy I have in my relationship with Him. Even when some days feel like a struggle, if I am choosing to seek Him each and every day, it does not matter what emotion befalls me. It is by His grace I have a constant peace in my heart that is, joy. This for me is true happiness, not the emotion that is stirred up based on things outside of myself that stimulate me within.

Regarding this truth, I can say that the scars of my past are real and many. Some have faded away, while others are in the process of fading, and yet others just may be part of my journey for the rest of my days here on earth. No matter my fate, my scars no longer define who I am, nor do they filter my eyes. My life experiences have developed me into who I am today, and they are very much a part of me; I am not a part of them. I don't stand within their shadows, nor are they shadows of my life. For the light that is God, has exposed them.

When I begin to doubt, I remember that who I am is someone who is "fearfully and wonderfully made."[6] With all my failures and with all my faults, I get to come as I am before the throne of Jesus to bow before my Maker. I thank Him for never letting me go and helping me realize that I was never rejected. I am His, and He is mine, and together I will continue to grow in this transformation that He has begun.

I pray that your heart is open to the truth that God is real, and that Jesus is the Messiah and only true source of power for healing, so that you too may learn that it is better to trust in the Lord than to put confidence in people or the things of this world.

- Ephesians 1:18 / Psalm 118:8

ENDNOTES

[1]   The apostle Paul talks about what it means to renew one's mind in Romans 12:2. It truly takes being vulnerable to surrender the pattern of thinking that points towards others as the source of our distress, especially when we have only known a dysfunctional cycle. A key indicator for me that I need to surrender is when I don't have peace in my heart. That moment just might be an opportunity to stop pointing the finger and to look within. It is amazing how when I take responsibility for my own instinctual reaction, that God becomes my focus, creating a space where His kingdom is more important than my own. Perspective!

[2]   The power of God is real and when we choose to believe, miracles do happen within our hearts. Our outside situation may not change the way we humanly desire, but the healing of our internal state is something that surpasses any condition in which we find ourselves. For a deeper reading on this, as my friend Karol pointed out, John 5 is an excellent choice.

[3]   The sermon that Jesus gave on a mountain is one of my favorite passages to read. I quoted from Matthew 7:13-14, which have been life verses for me.

[4]   Quoted from John 14:6

[5]   Philippians 4:11-12 talks about a godly joy, but I encourage you to read the whole book. Take your time and soak it in.

[6]   Quoted from Psalm 139:14

Printed in the United States
By Bookmasters